SKYLIGHTS

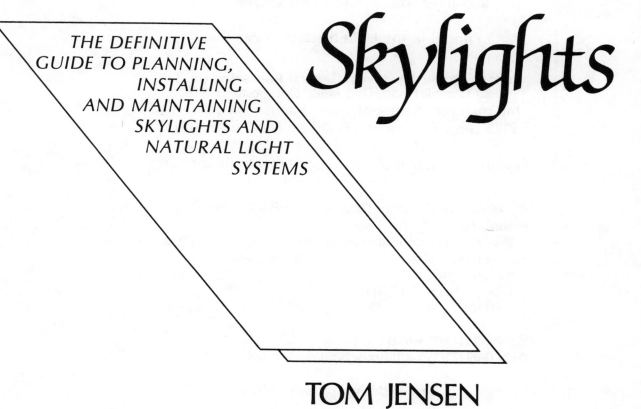

THE DEFINITIVE
GUIDE TO PLANNING,
INSTALLING
AND MAINTAINING
SKYLIGHTS AND
NATURAL LIGHT
SYSTEMS

Skylights

TOM JENSEN

Running Press
Philadelphia Pennsylvania

Printed in the United States of America.

Canadian representatives: General Publishing Co. Ltd.
30 Lesmill Road, Don Mills, Ontario M3B 2T6
International representatives: Kaiman & Polon, Inc.
2175 Lemoine Avenue, Fort Lee, New Jersey 07024
9   8   7   6   5   4   3
Digit on the right indicates the number of this printing.

Library of Congress Cataloging in Publication Data
Jensen, Tom.
   Skylights: the definitive guide to planning, installing, and
maintaining skylights and natural light systems.
   Includes index.
   1. Skylights.   1. Title.
   √ TH2487.J46   1983   690'.15   83-3089

ISBN 0-89471-194-6 (paperback)
ISBN 0-89471-195-4 (library binding)

Cover design by Jim Wilson
Front cover photograph: continuous vaulted skylight,
   courtesy of Naturalite, Inc.
Back cover photograph courtesy of Sunglo Skylight
   Products, Inc.
Illustrations by Suzanne Clee
Typography is Chelmsford (by Graphic Dimensions,
   Camden, NJ) and Zapf Chancery
Printed by Port City Press, Baltimore, MD

*This book may be ordered from the publisher. Please
include one dollar postage.* **But try your bookstore first.**

Running Press
125 South 22nd Street
Philadelphia, Pennsylvania 19103

TABLE OF CONTENTS

1 An Overview of Skylights

There simply isn't another home improvement or addition that can do what a skylight does. In *Walden,* Henry David Thoreau reminds us: "It would be well perhaps if we were to spend more of our days and nights without any obstruction between us and the celestial bodies." Bringing a view of the heavens into your home gives you not just blue sky and cumulus clouds, but the deep black night speckled with silver, and a chunk of the moon as well. Watching the Big Dipper move over your bed and then twist out of view, you can feel close to the natural cycles of dark and light.

Inviting a slice of sky into your home is not a new concept, of course. Ancient Romans used an atrium—an open garden area—to admit light into their houses. Unfortunately, those of us living in more northerly climates need a well-insulated, protective shelter that is closed to the elements.

The answer is a skylight, which *Webster's New Collegiate Dictionary* defines as "an opening in a house roof or ship's deck covered with translucent or transparent material and that is designed to admit light."

Just when glass was first used to cover a hole in a roof—and who put it there—we couldn't say. About the year 1 A.D., transparent glass sheets were first made in Rome. Venetians came to dominate the glass industry in the Middle Ages. In France, the first manufacture of plate glass in 1688 led to widespread use of mirrors and larger, stronger glass windows. Although plate glass did not become popular in America until 1850, window glass—made by spinning flat a bubble of blown glass—had been in great demand since the early eighteenth century.

The recent surge in skylight construction owes much to improvements in plastics. Acrylic plastic, commonly known as Plexiglas, is now readily available. Better acrylic bubbles, insulation, waterproof sealants, and pre-formed metal flashing have made it possible lately to welcome the sky into your home with only a moderate amount of time, money, and mechanical ability.

Modern technology has also broadened your choices. Notice that *Webster's* doesn't specify whether that skylight must be round or square, glass or plastic, small or multi-paned. Only cost and creativity limit the would-be skylighter's options.

So before you rush off to install your very own skylight, see what other people have already done. Our book presents and illustrates many ideas. If you still aren't certain what you want, check out skylight styles that regularly appear in magazines such as *Architectural Digest, House Beautiful, Better Homes and Gardens,* and *Country Home and Kitchen Ideas.*

More and more frequently, new homes feature skylights. Designers often use them as the central "theme" in a room. Older homes, too, can incorporate new skylights while preserving their classic architecture. Skylights are used in many commercial buildings as well as private residences; odds are your local shopping mall has large skylights to save on lighting costs. Factories and offices install skylights for the same reasons.

But beyond increased illumination, energy efficiency, and aesthetic improvement is the more practical profit motive. Industrial psychologists have demonstrated that workers who don't feel confined are more productive. Worker productivity also improves with a sense of environmental contact—and that's exactly what a skylight provides.

Obviously, a skylight's most important function is to let in the sun. But it's a mistake to

This wide skylight opens up a tight loft while giving the slumberer a panoramic view of the heavens.

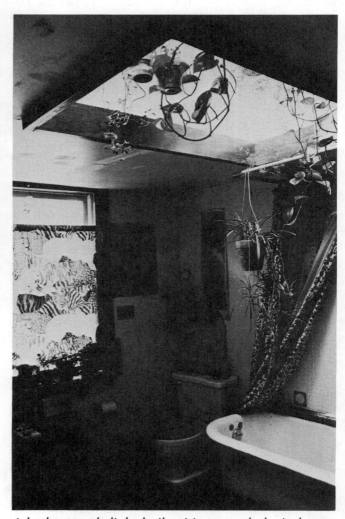

A bathroom skylight built with a recycled window.

Pre-formed plastic bubbles — in round or square styles — work best where you're chiefly interested in illumination. Their rounded contours and slight translucence tend to distort images and impede clear viewing.

Pre-formed plastic bubbles also blend in well with natural surroundings.

A contemporary plastic acrylic bubble.

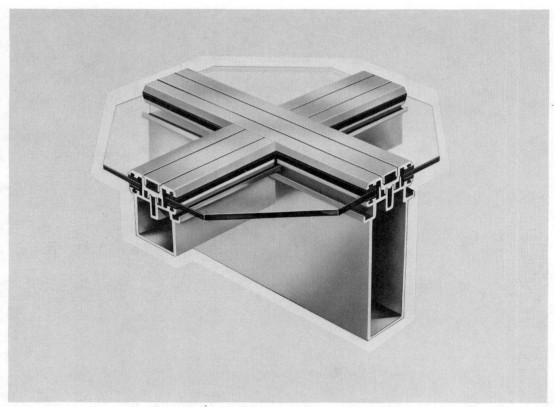

Tubular aluminum framing (above: courtesy Imperial Glass Structures) *allows for wide, strong, multi-paned skylights. Bottom diagram* (courtesy Fisher Skylights) *shows the components from below.*

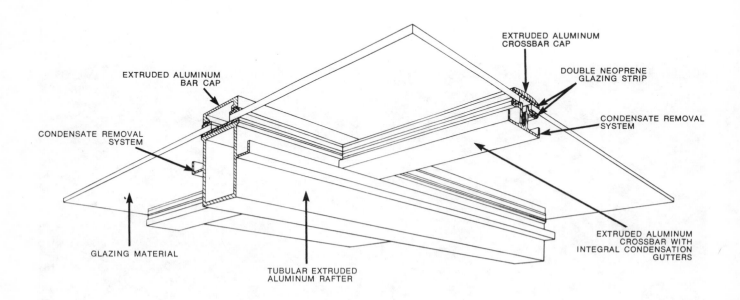

EXTRUDED ALUMINUM
CROSSBAR CAP

DOUBLE NEOPRENE
GLAZING STRIP

EXTRUDED ALUMINUM
BAR CAP

CONDENSATE REMOVAL
SYSTEM

CONDENSATE REMOVAL
SYSTEM

GLAZING MATERIAL

TUBULAR EXTRUDED
ALUMINUM RAFTER

EXTRUDED ALUMINUM
CROSSBAR WITH
INTEGRAL CONDENSATION
GUTTERS

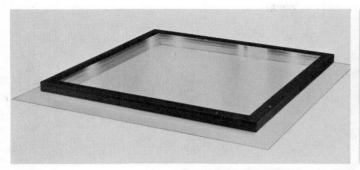
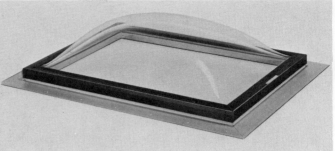

Three self-flashing, pre-fab skylights by Wasco. From top: fixed unit with safety glass, unit with acrylic plastic dome, and venting unit — also with safety glass.

think of a skylight as a hole that admits only sunlight. The skylight lets in *all* natural light. On a bright sunny day, your home will glow with warm radiance; the eerie calm of a full moon or a starry sky will lend itself to a quiet night of relaxation. (To capture the sun and moon, how-ever, you have to position your skylight prop-erly and decide during which seasons you want them to be visible.) And of course, one of Mother Nature's most spectacular sights is an intense electrical storm. The skylight can bring all these elements into your home, without

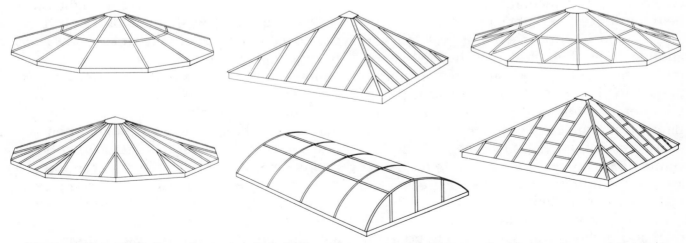

Framing allows, full three-dimensional skylights with great structural strength. Above, some multi-paned models from Fisher Skylights.

Plasticrafts' Winlite is essentially a vertical skylight, to be set as a porthole in an otherwise solid wall.

forcing you to sacrifice living space, comfort, or protection from the elements. (In the summertime, a skylight can be a mixed blessing, but in Chapter 12 we show you how to construct baffles and shades to minimize the problem of heat and glare. And our section on insulation covers the latest techniques and materials to help maximize a skylight's energy efficiency.)

As any interior decorator will tell you, another fringe benefit is that the well-lit area created by the skylight will increase your home's perceived size. By putting a dormant part of your home to work for you, a previously dull or dimly-lit corner can come alive. (One of the nicest uses for a skylight I've seen is in an 18th century barn converted to a private residence. Each of the upstairs bedrooms was treated to a massive 4' × 8' skylight.)

If you want to grow light-loving plants like cacti and orchids, you don't need to go to the expense and hassle of constructing a greenhouse. Instead, designate an area as a plant room, complete with a bank of skylights.

Are you a stained glass aficionado? You can show off a particularly nice specimen by mounting it in the ceiling. Watching its hues change according to the varying light that strikes it from above is spectacular.

But on a dark, moonless, rainy night, isn't a skylight kind of a washout? Not if you've recessed lighting into your skylight's shaftway. By turning on a switch from below, you can enjoy illumination 24 hours a day, no matter what the weather.

Without question, installing a skylight makes your home more desirable, often at a cost substantially lower than most other home improvements. For example, you can install a 48" × 48" skylight, no matter how complex its design, for less money than it would take to carpet an average-sized living room, wallpaper a kitchen, or paint your house's exterior.

Of course you can spend a small fortune on a pre-fabricated, custom-built skylight, but

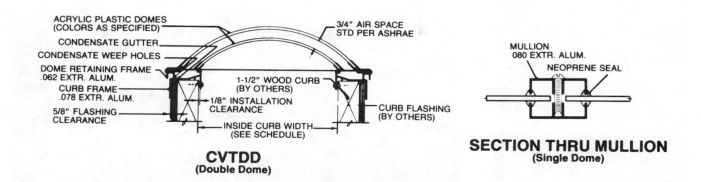

ACRYLIC PLASTIC DOMES
(COLORS AS SPECIFIED)

3/4" AIR SPACE
STD PER ASHRAE

CONDENSATE GUTTER

CONDENSATE WEEP HOLES

DOME RETAINING FRAME
.062 EXTR. ALUM.

CURB FRAME
.078 EXTR. ALUM.

1-1/2" WOOD CURB
(BY OTHERS)

1/8" INSTALLATION
CLEARANCE

5/8" FLASHING
CLEARANCE

CURB FLASHING
(BY OTHERS)

INSIDE CURB WIDTH
(SEE SCHEDULE)

CVTDD
(Double Dome)

MULLION
080 EXTR. ALUM.

NEOPRENE SEAL

SECTION THRU MULLION
(Single Dome)

Blueprint for Naturalite's continuous vault skylight, depicted on this book's front cover.

A renovated loft, using skylights to emphasize the texture of walls and floors.

Room enclosure by Lynbrook Glass.

Acrylic venting units by APC Corporation, arranged symmetrically along the peak of a roof.

you don't *have* to. "Shall we forever resign the pleasure of construction to the carpenter?" Thoreau asked. "What does architecture amount to in the experience of men? I never in all my walks came across a man engaged in so simple and natural an occupation as building his house." Some part of that pleasure will be yours when you cut a hole in your roof and set down the glass.

This book will show how you, the weekend carpenter, can build and install a simple, inexpensive skylight in one day using only basic tools and skills—without going broke or crazy in the process. When you consider the minimal effort involved, it's a wonder that more people don't have skylights.

Is your budget enough to let you put in several Plexiglas bubbles? No problem: that's covered, too, along with a complete list of their manufacturers.

If you can conceive it and afford it, odds are you can do it yourself. The sun's glow in your living room on a cold day in January will be a welcome sight. And should you ever decide to sell your residence, the initial outlay for your skylight will be repaid—with interest.

A skylight offers extra light—and visibility—to hanging plants and stained glass pendants.

This urban horticulturalist has tilted his acrylic skylight to the south to trap as much sun as possible.

An angled skylight by Lynbrook Glass acts like a dormer window—but is far easier to install.

2 Planning Your Skylight

The most important part of *any* home improvement project is taking the time to think it out properly. It doesn't take a great deal of money or carpentry skills to bring the sky into your home, but it *does* require careful planning and attention to detail. Good skylight installation is not a matter of luck; you must give careful thought to the placement, the expense (both in time and money), and the construction plan.

Before even thinking about purchasing any supplies or beginning construction, the novice skylighter is best advised to read this entire book, and learn how to do it right. A skylight offers many different ideas and possibilities. There could be ideas you hadn't thought of, or available techniques and materials that you weren't even aware of. Not sure whether you really want to build your own skylight? Reading about the work involved will help you make up your mind. And since some tasks do overlap, it's a good idea to know *all* that needs to be done before doing *any* construction. Familiarizing yourself with the information lets you make a decision that will best suit your needs, taste, budget, and mechanical aptitude.

CHOOSING A LOCATION

For some people, the toughest part of the decision is not where to put a skylight, but where *not* to put one. Slightly different locations for a skylight can produce widely different effects, so consider as many situations as possible. You, and only you, can decide what you want a skylight to be and what you want it to do for you. Once you have decided to admit natural light into your home, it makes sense to use the skylight as a functional part of a design that makes the best use of your home's existing light, decor, and structure. Any skylight is better than none, but you want to have your room look like it was built around your skylight, instead of the other way around.

Walk around the inside of your home. Which rooms might benefit from being brightened up or having the ceiling "raised"? In a bathroom, for example, the combination of natural light and high humidity helps houseplants flourish. A skylight over a stairway or a gloomy corner is a natural brightener. If you feel your attic bedroom is too small, a dormer-skylight will let in a chunk of the universe. Even if your roof is shaded by trees or other buildings, you'll be surprised at the amount of reflected light a skylight can bring in.

In the Northern Hemisphere, the brightest light comes from the south and the west. You can figure out the geographical placement of your home in any of three ways: 1) look at your home's original blueprints and get the direction from them, 2) use a pocket compass, or 3) interpolate the placement of your home from the position of the sun. It rises in the east

In this special construction by Lynbrook Glass, the skylight extends down from the roof to join a matching window.

A humid bathroom, brightened by a skylight, provides the ideal environment for houseplants.

and sets in the west, and at noon, casts shadows toward the north. This knowledge will help you finalize your skylight's placement. For more light, place your skylight where it has southern exposure. Want less light? Put it on a north side —or to the west or east for afternoon or morning light, respectively. (Multiple skylights are becoming more popular for just this reason.)

WHAT'S YOUR ROOF LIKE?

Once you decide where you want the skylight to be on the inside of your house; take a look outside and see what materials cover the roof. Wood, asphalt and asbestos shingles, tile or slate, and materials like tin, aluminum, copper, and galvanized iron are most common

on a pitched roof. For a flat or low-pitched roof, the covering generally used is roofing felt,, built up in layers and topped with gravel.

Slate and tile roofs may not be suitable for a home-built skylight, because they require specialized tools. If you have either of these roof types, contact your builder or a local contractor for specific recommendations. But for all other roof coverings, you will be able to use the curb and flashing method with no difficulty.

Your skylight planning must take into account some intangibles as well. To see how a skylight will look on your home's exterior, make a frame of it (use the curb) and place it on the roof. This crude approximation of the finished product can indicate whether the sym-

Lynbrook Glass' tubular framing allows a unique view of lower Fifth Avenue.

metry of your exterior will be disturbed. There is no inherently incorrect spot for the skylight, but ideally, it should harmonize with the outside as well.

Examine your trees, too. Could limbs fall and damage a skylight? If so, avoid using plate glass and stick with Plexiglas, which is far less likely to shatter. Plexiglas is also the best choice for high-vandalism areas. It can be scratched and nicked, but to shatter it takes a force far greater than that of a thrown rock. But if, after reading this book, you decide that plate glass is the only substance you'd be happy with, cut down the offending limbs *before* beginning your roof work.

Next, a thorough inspection of your roof is in order. What kind of shape is it in? Does the roofing material appear intact? Does it need new shingles or new flashing? How about the gutters—are they clean and still firmly attached? Gutters that have to be unclogged every autumn are a needless annoyance. Since you're up on the roof anyway, now is the perfect time to install gutter screening. It's cheap, readily available at hardware stores, and snaps in place in a jiffy. You can do an average-sized house in less than a half hour—and spend your fall weekends watching football instead of cleaning gutters. If you are going to put in a skylight, it makes sense to kill two birds with one stone, and do any needed roof repairs at the same time.

UP ON THE ROOF

The thought of climbing around on the roof shouldn't deter you from building a skylight. If you learn a few roof rules and follow them, you'll have a beautiful skylight and a job safely done.

The best footwear for roof walking is a good pair of work boots with steel toes and solid rubber soles. Stay away from jogging shoes or sneakers. They give excellent traction, but are useless (as I discovered) when someone drops a five-pound sledge on your foot. I've sworn off jogging shoes on the roof; two fractured toes are enough.

If you're alone on a section of roof accessible only by ladder, keep someone within earshot. I once got stuck on a roof after my ladder fell. No one was around to put it back up—or to hear me curse.

The last thing you want is a Three Stooges side-step that takes you straight down. Try to develop the little trick of spotting where you are going to put your feet *before* you put them there. It may save a nasty spill or terrifying slide. Stepping on anything not securely anchored is bound to upset your traction and/or balance, so make certain there's no loose debris where you're about to plant your foot. And while standing on the roof, try not to put all your weight on one foot. I went through one that way!

As a card-carrying acrophobic, I used to regard roof walking with a mixture of fear and

These swiveled skylights by APC Corporation open to admit fresh air plus sunlight, and clean up quickly.

loathing. Naturally, my fear of roofs increased in direct proportion to the height and steepness of the surface I was working on. Being ten feet off the ground on a low-pitched roof is not bad at all. Being fifty or sixty feet up, on a roof pitched like a church steeple, can give you religion in a hurry. But when your livelihood depends on negotiating treacherous roofs, you quickly learn how to maneuver with minimal problems. And you avoid walking on damp roofs until they have dried fully.

Remember, on a roof, *gravity works with you, not against you.* On the surface, that statement seems nonsensical. After all, since you are up in the air, doesn't gravity attempt to pull you down? Well, gravity does exert a downward force. But it doesn't try to pull you *off* the roof,

A roof, as seen from below. Each nail is a possible source of leaks.

it pulls you *closer* to the roof. Without going into the physics involved, you'll adhere better to the roof if your body weight is close to its surface. When you're on a steep section of roof, be sure to lean your body flat against the surface to the roof. Do not attempt to stand erect! Keep your weight as close as possible to the top of the roof.

The above technique is great if you get stuck in a high place, or are unsure of your footing. To lower yourself gradually, move slowly to the side, keeping your arms spread wide, and using your knees and hands as pivoting points. As you move laterally, angle your descent at an approximately 45-degree pitch. Remember to keep your body close to the shingles, and don't make any sharp movements.

Shingles can get hot, even on mild days. If you plan to spend much time on the roof, buy a set of knee pads. You'll save wear and tear on your knees—and on the roof itself.

Lastly, keep your hospitalization and disability insurance paid up. My next-door neighbor fell from the second-floor roof to the garage roof, to the ground. He broke his back, fractured his skull and, as a result, was out of work and saddled with expensive medical bills that he couldn't pay. But to some people, just the thought of being on the roof is terrifying. If that is the case with you, hire someone to do the inspection and construction for you.

Don't confine the inspection to the outside of the building. If there's an attic, go up

A metal grid facilitates plant-hanging in this skylight.

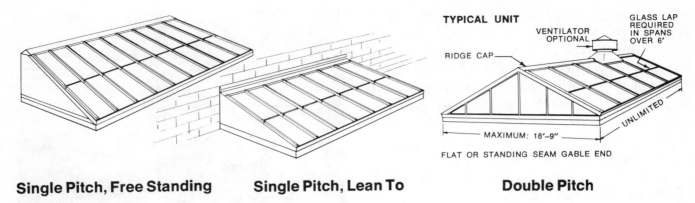

Single Pitch, Free Standing   **Single Pitch, Lean To**   **Double Pitch**

For flat-roofed buildings, Fisher Skylights' multi-paned units offer generous illumination.

and check the structural soundness of the beams and the inside of the roof—especially under where you'll be walking. But be careful in unfinished attics. Walking on joists can be tricky, especially if your sense of balance is suspect. Never step directly on insulation; it's almost always supported by drywall alone, which will *not* support anyone's weight. Serious injuries have a decidedly negative impact on the enjoyment quotient of any project. So

place one or two sturdy boards perpendicular to the joists and step carefully on them.

While you should inspect *all* of the roof, inside and out, pay especially close attention to the location of your proposed skylight. Look for signs of rot, termites, moisture, and wear. While installing a skylight in one old home, I was appalled to discover that the 4" × 4" beams supporting the roof had nearly rotted away. Some were less than half an inch thick! The

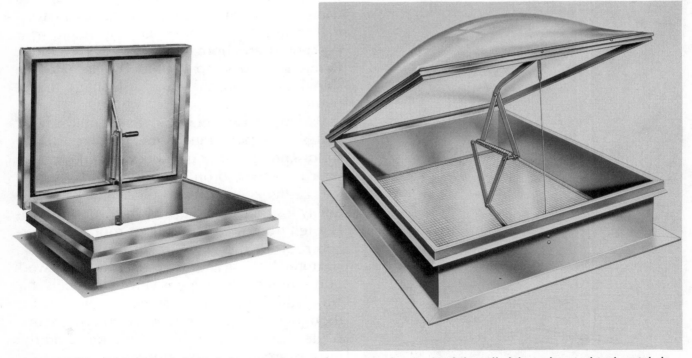

Naturalite's Roof Scuttle skylight (left) provides easy access to the roof, while Hillsdale Industries' industrial skylights (right) are hinged to allow venting of heat, fumes, and dust.

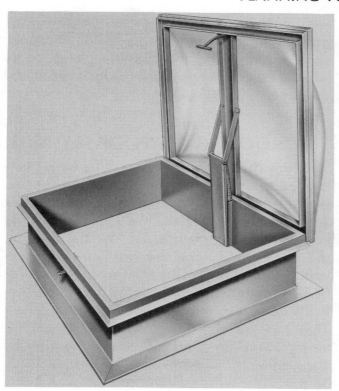

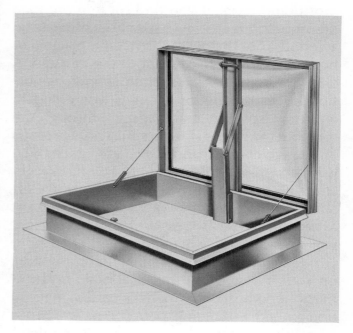

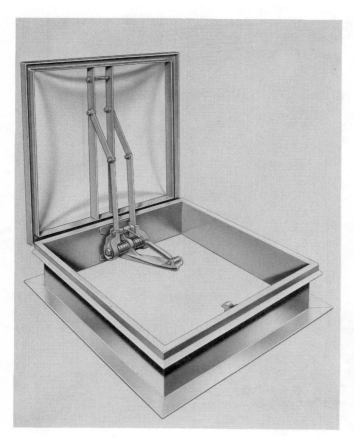

roof was barely able to support *itself,* let alone any major structural changes. The problem was resolved only through complete structural renovation and several heated visits from the building inspector. Still, it's better to fix things the right way, than to fall through the roof (which, I can assure you from experience, is no fun) or even worse, to have the roof collapse.

Naturally, problems like these tend to be much more severe in older buildings, but it's better to be safe than sorry. You can test if any of the inside roof is rotten by probing it lightly with a screwdriver. If the wood is soft, DO NOT WALK ON IT! It has already started to decay.

The skylight's function is not to serve as a repair patch for a badly leaking or rotted section of the roof. Roof leaks should be fixed *before* the skylight goes in, for the simple reason that where the water drips on the inside is often not where it originally came in from the outside. Frequently, water will run down rafters for a great distance before revealing itself.

You must determine *where* the water *enters* the house. Look for tears in the coverings or for nails that have popped up. Check carefully around the chimney's flashing and around protruding vents. If you find rot in more than one spot, odds are you have either a bad leak, an entire roof that will soon need replacing, or both. Determine the extent of the damage. A decaying roof is best repaired as soon as possible, because the problem is not going to improve. Not only could you fall through the roof, but the whole structure may be weakened enough to collapse under heavy weight or high winds. Many people decide to build a skylight *after* discovering they need a new roof. Certainly nothing's wrong with that logic; it's just as easy (in many cases easier) to put in a skylight while a new roof is being installed.

One last thing: before beginning any work on your skylight, call the local building commissioner or inspector to make certain that you don't need a building permit—or if you *do* need one, find out how to apply. Nine times out of ten, you won't need a permit. But since state, county, and local building codes vary widely, you can save yourself a lot of grief and money by checking ahead.

CHOOSING A TYPE OF SKYLIGHT

Now that you've completed the basic planning steps, you are ready to choose a specific skylight—and as noted earlier, the possibilities are almost limitless. Here, we will concern ourselves with three basic styles: the flat skylight, the box skylight, and the pre-fabricated skylight. Although you'll find some esoteric or one-of-a-kind skylights, almost all home skylights belong to one of these three categories. They have several things in common: each is versatile, elegant, and can be put together by the weekend carpenter.

This pre-fab bubble by APC Corporation includes its own curb and flashing, reducing installation time.

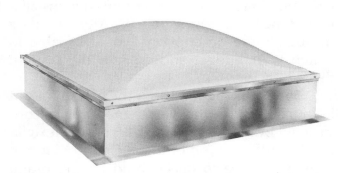

Naturalite's factory-assembled skylight features an insulated metal curb and one-piece, acrylic plastic dome.

How much do you want to spend? To help you figure the eventual cost, break down the job of erecting the skylight into its component projects, each with its own materials. First there is the erection of the curb, needed for all the skylights you can construct and for most commercially manufactured skylights as well. (If you're installing a ready-made skylight, consult the instructions provided with it.)

Your second step is to figure which type of skylight to use. Remember, the manufactured variety can be two and three times as expensive as your own would be. For example, for the price of a 24" × 24" pre-fab skylight, you can put in a *complete* 48" × 48" skylight, curb included, and probably still have a few dollars left over.

The aluminum angle used to seal and hold the skylight in place can be bought in any good hardware store. For caulking, I recommend strongly that you spend the extra money for silicone caulk made by either DuPont or General Electric. The cost is worthwhile, considering how long it lasts.

The last step in estimating the cost is determining how the inside of the skylight will look. Because of all the possibilities, you should take the time to decide what you really want. If the ceiling of the room is the roof of the house (as in an attic, or a top-floor room where the ceiling has been removed), then there isn't much for you to do. On the other hand, if your skylight has to pierce a ceiling as well as the

roof, don't worry—there are easy ways to frame in that shaftway and finish it attractively (see Chapter 11).

Framing requires fairly expensive materials. Of course, using costly wall covering or lights in the shaft will shoot the price up, too. But some wall coverings that might be prohibitively expensive for larger areas may do just right here.

Drywall can be installed to match the ceiling. Lights installed in the shaft will bring a pleasant, diffused glow into the room. If plants are going in the shaft, you might want to put in wood paneling or cover the walls in burlap.

Whichever type of skylight you choose, you will need a plan. If you are doing the work

The shafts of these twin skylights by Lynbrook Glass have been finished with drywall, to match the ceiling.

yourself, the plan need be no more than a rough sketch to help you envision what you're after. But if you are having the skylight built by someone else, every detail should be resolved with the builder before work is begun. You must have a firm, detailed idea of the skylight's location and how it should be trimmed. Unanticipated changes always increase the cost, and you'll save money in the long run by avoiding them. And if you are considering a manufactured skylight, check out the manufacturers in Appendix A at the end of this book.

Before you make a final decision on which skylight is best for you, though, read through the upcoming sections on materials and installation techniques. As you might expect, each skylight type has pros and cons, so we'll discuss each one in terms of cost, complexity, installation time, and appearance. After reading through these descriptions, you'll be able to match your budget and skills to the skylight that's best for you.

The flat skylight is by far the easiest for do-it-yourselfers. As the name implies, it is constructed by simply laying a flat sheet of Plexiglas or plate glass on top of the curb. Aluminum is angled over the corners to hold it in place, and it's sealed with high-grade silicone caulk to prevent water from entering.

Flat skylights have several advantages over other types. They're the least expensive: you can build and install a complete 4' × 4' flat

Cutaway drawing of a Stargazer Skylight by Imperial Glass Structures shows how flashing (in white) fits over the wooden curb and under the roofing material.

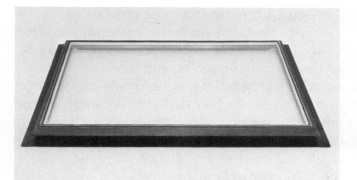

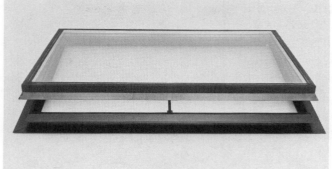

Lynbrook's low-profile, all-glass skylights come in fixed and vented models.

skylight for approximately $100.

Flat skylights allow tremendous flexibility. You can use almost any type of flat, transparent material: stained glass, clear or tinted Plexiglas, or translucent ("frosted") Plexiglas, which admits only diffuse light. Many people use thermal glass—two layers of glass with a vacuum or boundary layer of air in between—to serve as insulation. Use your imagination and you'll be able to come up with still other interesting possibilities.

True, a flat skylight does have a few drawbacks. It involves more work than a pre-fab unit, although that isn't (and shouldn't be) a prohibitive difference. A person with average mechanical aptitude should be able to install a flat skylight in one day at the most. This type is no more complex than the box skylight, but is the only type constructed with glass, and so can be broken unless you use a guard (see Chapter 14). But the flat skylight's biggest shortcoming is

its rather crude exterior appearance, particularly when compared to a pre-fab unit. This may not be a major concern if you live on the top floor of an inner-city building, but it is a point worth pondering. But since no type of skylight looks inherently better from *below*, your choice will not affect the view from inside.

Whether you use Plexiglas or plate glass for a flat skylight, using an extra layer of thermal glass will keep heat loss to a minimum. But because of the cost and because there's another way to insulate the skylight itself, I don't recommend using thermal glass. For extra insulation, consult Chapter 11 for all you need to know about internal storm windows.

The Plexiglas box skylight is a different answer to the same question: namely, how do you cover your curb? In principle, it works much like a hat. A box is constructed from Plexiglas, dropped over the curb, and fastened with screws. No aluminum angle is necessary,

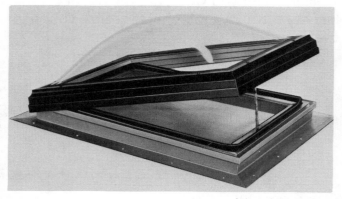

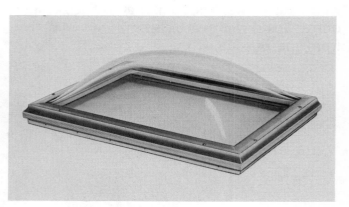

Venting and fixed acrylic bubbles, manufactured by Wasco.

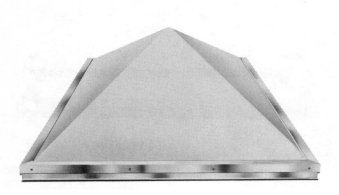

Naturalite's pyramidal pre-fab unit in translucent plastic.

because the sides of the Plexiglas box hang down over the curb.

In cost and complexity, it's similar to the flat skylight. The difference is that some people don't like having to glue the Plexiglas to form the box, and don't feel confident that the joints will hold together. Knowing what you're doing, of course, eliminates both problems. Read through the construction and installation sections for both types, and decide which would be easiest for *you*.

On the minus side, box skylights are unfortunately the least flexible of the three types. Plexiglas is the only material you can use—to duplicate this effect in glass would be difficult, since the sides of the box have to support the weight of the top. You can always use tinted Plexiglas, or install an inner shade, but you won't have the freedom that a flat skylight offers. Box skylights are also the least attractive from the outside. If this is a concern to you,

then go with either a flat or pre-fab.

The pre-fab skylight, far and away the most costly of the three types, is used primarily by professional contractors, and by do-it-yourselfers who lack the time, skills, or self-confidence to build a flat or box skylight. Typically, a pre-fab unit costs up to four times as much as a flat or box skylight. Its main attractions are that the work involved in installation is minimal, and the options *extremely* varied.

All you need do is cut a hole in the roof, build a curb, and attach the pre-fab unit—a matter of a couple of hours, instead of an entire day. And skylight manufacturers put out an almost endless number of designs, the most common of which is the bubble. But there are also some flat pre-fabs, as well as domes, triangles, and other shapes. If a particular pattern appeals to you, fine, but keep in mind that you can also create such a design if you build the skylight yourself.

Perhaps a pre-fab skylight's most desirable aspect is its appearance. It's certainly the best choice if you're fussy about your house's looks and aren't fazed by the corresponding premium in price. Appendix A lists manufacturers of pre-fab skylights, as well as tips on what to look for.

Even if you are planning to install a pre-fab skylight, it would be a good idea to read the rest of this book first. Manufacturers' instructions, while sometimes complete, tend to oversimplify the installation process. By familiarizing yourself with the material in this book, you can prepare yourself for all phases of skylight installation, and you won't run the risk of getting halfway through a job only to realize you're in over your head.

3 Preparations for Doing It Yourself

*I*t takes less time to design and follow a plan than it does to throw something together and have to do the whole project again later. I've seen jobs that had to be done over completely, at considerable cost in time, money, and frustration—all because someone didn't follow the directions. The secret to a job well-done is *not* having twenty years of carpentry experience; it's taking the time to read and follow directions, and paying close attention to detail.

PICKING THE RIGHT TIME

One aspect of skylight installation that is often inexplicably overlooked is *when* to do the job. Working on black asphalt shingles when the temperature hits 95 degrees is no fun. And when it's ten degrees below zero, you have the added difficulty of a slippery, frozen surface to stand on. If you install a skylight in below-freezing temperatures, frozen water can expand and crack the wood, causing monumental leaks.

The best time to cut the hole in your roof (and expose your house's interior to the elements for eight hours or so) is either in spring or fall, when you're free from extremes of heat and cold, and the outside temperature is between sixty and seventy-five degrees.

If you put a skylight in during winter, you will lose most of the heat from the house—so wait a few months and save on your heating bill. And if you work in the summer and your home is air-conditioned, expect substantial cooling losses. Even if you turn off the air conditioning, opening the roof will allow the cool air inside to escape. And it will take much longer (and cost more) to recool your home.

If the climate makes you rush your work, you may do a haphazard job and be haunted by the end result. Remember: you need only about eight hours to work, but the skylight will be with you for as long as you live in your house. Allow yourself enough time.

Other temperature-related problems to watch out for are the curing times for roof cement and caulk. The directions for these adhesives specify the range of temperatures they should be used in. If your caulk is not recommended for use below forty degrees, then don't use it below forty degrees! A point like this seems obvious, yet neophyte carpenters sometimes fail to read or follow the instructions, and pay for their transgressions with severe leaks. Always apply adhesives in the proper temperature range and give them adequate time to dry.

When scheduling your skylight work, check the long-range weather forecasts. Ideally, you should have *three* days—the day before to dry out the roof, the day of construction, and the day after to give the roof cement time to dry

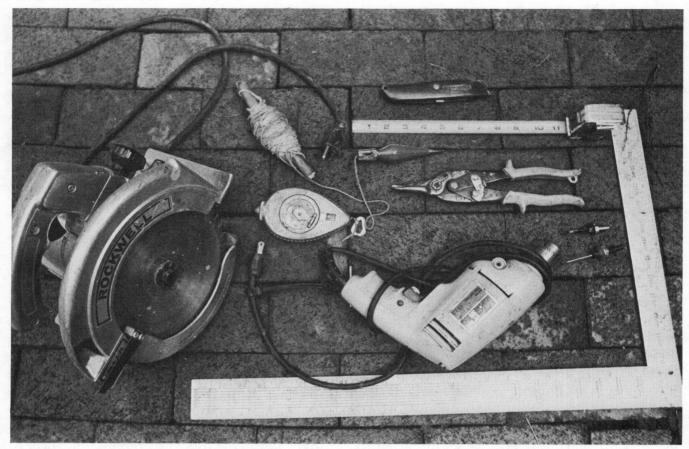

A skylighter's basic tools. From top to bottom: utility knife, tape measure, plumb bob, tin snips, chalk line, power saw, power drill, drill bits, aluminum framing square.

and set up. This is not always possible, particularly in high-moisture areas, but the longer you can avoid rain, the better off you'll be. Keep an eye on the humidity as well: the dryer the air, the faster adhesives will cure.

At the very least, allow one full day for skylight installation. It won't take the whole day in most instances, but leaving yourself extra time lets you fix any minor problems that crop up without resorting to ineffective, quickie solutions. Again, give yourself time to do it right!

POWER AND HAND TOOLS FOR SKYLIGHT INSTALLATION

Before construction begins, it's a good idea to examine the tools you'll need to do the job correctly. The tools required for skylight installation are basic; many people have them already. If you're missing any items, however, avoid time-consuming delays by borrowing or purchasing the tools ahead of time.

Here's an alphabetized checklist of what you'll want to have handy.

Essential Hand Tools

1. *Chalk line* is used for marking lines. With one kind, the chalk comes in a small block and is run along the string. The best type is self-contained, with the line on a spool and powdered chalk in the line itself. Refills are available at nominal cost. This unit may also be used as a plumb bob. Its only drawback is that occasionally it will snag if you wind up the line too quickly. Take your time and you won't have a problem.

2. *Chisel*—a ¾" blade is sufficient.

3. *Flooring chisel,* also known as an electrician's chisel, is a heavy-duty chisel with a 2½" blade. You'll need it to cut sheet metal and pry up roofing material.

4. *Framing square* is used for laying out studs, drawing straight lines, and cutting drywall. Leave wood and plastic squares to the tenderfoots. Aluminum framing squares won't rust, bend, or break under anything less than superhuman stress. Purchase a well-built one and you'll never have to worry about buying another.

5. *Hammer*—you want a good 16 oz. hammer with a straight or curved claw.

6. *Hand saw* is measured by the teeth (called points) per inch. An 8-point saw is the proper one to use. Make sure the blade is sharp; a dull blade makes cutting twice as hard. In addition, getting a precise cut—crucial for this job—is more difficult because a dull saw moves erratically.

7. *Level*—a good one is cheap insurance against putting in the curb crookedly.

8. *Plumb bob*—a heavy, weighted object on a string, used for marking vertical lines. You can make one inexpensively by tying twine to a heavy, cone-shaped fishing sinker.

9. *Pry bar,* commonly known as a crowbar, is valuable because it performs a number of functions. As the name implies, it is perfect for prying loose objects like roofing material. And because it gives you much more leverage than the traditional claw hammer (see above), it's also great for removing hard-to-get-out nails.

10. *Ruler*—an 8- or 12-foot metal tape measure is your best bet. Cheaper cloth or plastic tapes can twist or deform, making it difficult to get accurate measurements.

11. *Screwdrivers*—two straight-blade: one 8", and one 4", and one Phillips screwdriver with a #2 point.

12. *Tin snips*—a must for cutting flashing painlessly. Ordinary hand-held garden shears will be adequate, as long as they're sharp.

13. *Utility or mat knife* is the carpenter's equivalent of a Cuisinart: it cuts, slices, and chops with effortless efficiency. Sturdy and inexpensive, utility knives are great for slicing shingles, drywall, and even flashing. When you purchase one, be sure to buy five or six spare blades, too. No matter how careful you are, they do snap from time to time, and you don't want to interrupt your work to get new blades.

Plumb bobs are particularly handy for marking the sides of a vertical shaftway.

With these basic tools, the weekend carpenter and would-be skylighter will have everything necessary to do a professional job that'll bring much satisfaction and sunlight into a home. The only thing to watch out for is poor quality. *DON'T EVER BUY CHEAP TOOLS!* They spoil your work and are not safe. A hammerhead that flies off in mid-swing could severely damage your project, or worse, yourself.

Most of the hand tools I use are ten to fifteen years old, and I have had few problems with them. A *true* bargain is a tool that performs quality work, lasts a long time, *and* is reasonable in price. If a tool does not meet the first two criteria, then it's no bargain. Save yourself grief: invest the time and money to get tools that will last a lifetime.

If you're unsure about which are best, inquire at a hardware store for recommendations. Occasionally, however, salespeople will pitch a particular brand because it's the only line they carry, or because they are trying to move a slow-selling item. The best way, then, is to ask a professional carpenter or contractor what he uses. A person who makes his living with tools will not hesitate to tell you which brands hold up and which don't.

Just because a particular tool is the top of its class doesn't mean you have to spend a fortune on it. There's no sense paying top dollar when a little sharp hunting can get you something at a discount. Once you decide on a brand and model, shop around carefully. One advantage of today's tough economic times is that it's a buyer's marketplace, and you'll be surprised at how much money you can save.

Though hand tools require little maintenance, you shouldn't ignore or abuse them. Salts and minerals found in common soil, for instance, can badly corrode even high-quality tools. If your tools get dirty, wipe them clean to avoid rust and deterioration, and store them in a dry place.

HELPFUL POWER TOOLS

Many a weekend carpenter believes that to do a job right, he needs enough power tools to erect a skyscraper. For most skylight installations, all you *really* need are a ¼" drill, and a circular saw. A ⅜" drill is a bit sturdier than a ¼"

drill. But unless you plan on drilling into cement walls or using your drill 40 hours a week, a ¼" one is more than adequate.

The same applies to circular saws. Unless you're a professional carpenter, you don't need one of those ultra-heavy-duty power saws that can cut through steel and remain sharp enough to filet roast beef. A medium-grade, brandname saw is all you'll probably ever need—and it's priced more reasonably than a professional saw.

A belt sander is a nice convenience, but not a necessity. Any sanding you'll need to do can be done by hand. In fact, you should sand Plexiglas by hand to avoid cracking the ends. If you think you'll need a sander for future projects, purchase one. But if not, save yourself thirty-five dollars or so and use it for other essentials—like beer and pizza to celebrate your finished skylight masterpiece.

Power tools should be chosen with even more care than hand tools, if for no other reason than their higher cost. Using price as a guideline, you can pretty well figure out what you are buying. But when you get set to buy any power tool, decide what you need it for. If you aren't going to do any major renovation work and the projects you intend to work on aren't too large, then the cheaper, light-duty power tools may do just fine. On the other hand, if you're going to put tools through the rigors of house renovation or heavy-duty building, it's worth it to spend the extra money for appropriate tools. Again, the best advertising is word of mouth. Talk to a contractor to find out what he uses. If a power tool holds up under the heavy day-to-day duress that a professional gives it, you can be certain it will serve you well in your home carpentry forays.

One clue of a tool's quality is the type of bearing in the motor. Needle and roller bearings are much better than bronze bushings, but bronze bushings will work okay if kept well oiled. But in determining the quality of the tool, there is one chief thing to look for: *amps versus horsepower.* Every electric motor is rated in amperage; the higher the amps, the better the motor. If *only* the tool's horsepower is listed, you can suspect that the amps are lower than they should be. A motor may have what seems like a good horsepower rating, but it may burn out prematurely if the amp rating does not correspond. Horsepower and amp ratings vary for different tools and for different uses. See the chart at right to help figure the correct ratings.

Amperes / Horsepower	Light duty		Heavy duty	
¼" Drill	1.5	½	2.5	½
⅜" Drill	2.5	¾	3.5	¾
7¼" Circular Handsaw	7.5	1½	8.5	2
8¼" Circular Handsaw	9.0	1¾	12.0	2
Router	3.1	¾	8.0	1½
Orbital Sander	1.5	½	3.0	1
Belt Sander	6.0	1.5	10.5	2.0
Saber or Bayonet Saw	2.3	¼	3.5	½

Need a good, inexpensive toolbox? Plywood or scrap lumber cut to these dimensions will do the trick.

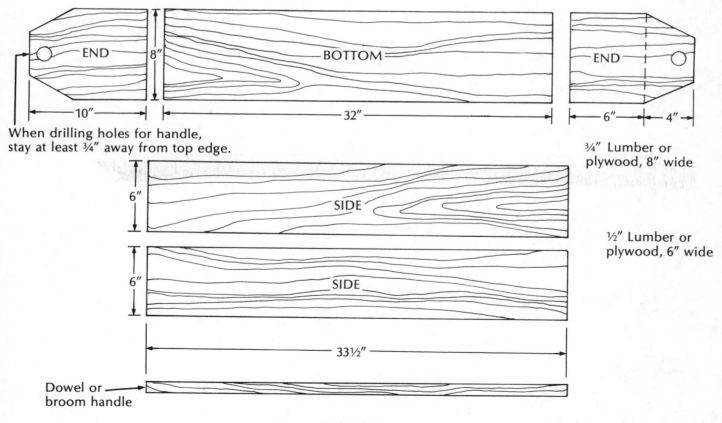

END 8" BOTTOM END

10" 32" 6" 4"

When drilling holes for handle, stay at least ¾" away from top edge.

¾" Lumber or plywood, 8" wide

SIDE 6"

SIDE 6"

½" Lumber or plywood, 6" wide

33½"

Dowel or broom handle

FIGURE 1

A CONVENIENT, COMPACT TOOL BOX

When you have all your tools together, get a place to stash 'em. Building a good box is so simple that it is well worth the effort — and will last you a lifetime. The best material to use is ¾" and ½" plywood, though you can also use packing crates. Nails will work for fastening, but 1¼" #8 wood screws (W.S.) and glue are best. If you have any waterproof glue, dig it out. If not, Elmer's will do just fine.

The base and ends should be made of ¾" wood. Since the ends and bottom are the same width, they can be cut from the same piece of lumber. One-half inch is right for the sides and the compartment dividers you may want to add for general and special tools. Use your router to dado the corners. The handle can be cut from an old broom or mop. If you buy a dowel, get one that feels comfortable in your hand.

Any box longer than 32" will be a little hard to manage. The ends should be about 10" high; the sides about 5½". The measurements for this box are average, but look at your tools and build your box accordingly.

Our box in the picture (Figure 2) has three compartments: one for saws, the second for regular hand tools, and a third smaller section for rulers, chalk lines, sharpening stone, etc. I usually keep things I don't want bounced around in that third section. Along the middle of the box, I sectioned the center divider to store screwdrivers and chisels. The divider is made out of ½" stock (to keep the weight down). Since it is difficult to nail into an end of that width, I used blocks to nail the divider to, and a ¾" square block which runs the full length of each corner.

TOP VIEW of Tool box, showing suggested compartments

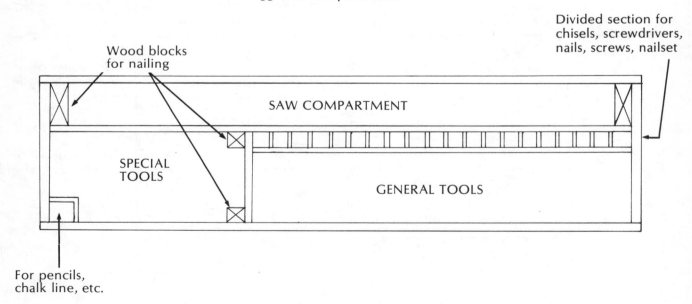

Divided section for chisels, screwdrivers, nails, screws, nailset

Wood blocks for nailing

SAW COMPARTMENT

SPECIAL TOOLS

GENERAL TOOLS

For pencils, chalk line, etc.

FIGURE 2

After you have collected your materials, including screws and glue, then cut all pieces to size. Cut the angles in the ends and drill the handle holes, making sure there is enough material to hold so that the handle will not pull out of either end. Next glue and screw the ends to the bottom. (A screw set in the drill makes the installation of the screws easier and better.) Make the dividers before you put the sides on, since it's easier to work without the sides. Use wood blocks for spacers. We used the ½" wood, cut into strips, for the sectioned divider down

the tool box's center. After putting in all your dividers, screw and glue the sides to the base and ends. Install the dowel handle by nailing through the dowel from the top of the end. Put in your tools—and get ready to build a skylight.

If you want to employ dado joints [see inset], then the box's sides, bottom, and ends should all be of ¾" wood. Depth of the dados should be ⅜" — exactly half the thickness of the material — and should all be cut in the end pieces, not in the sides or bottom.

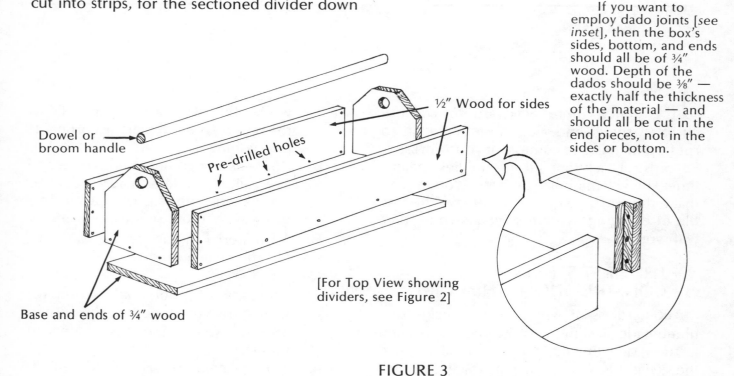

Dowel or broom handle

Pre-drilled holes

½" Wood for sides

Base and ends of ¾" wood

[For Top View showing dividers, see Figure 2]

FIGURE 3

4 Preliminary Construction

It is much more awkward to construct curbs, flashing, and aluminum angle on the rooftop than in the comfort of your workshop. So construct all your sub-assemblies ahead of time. This will minimize time spent on the roof, make the work go quicker, and save the trouble of dragging every tool you own up there with you.

THE FIRST STEP IN CONSTRUCTION: THE CURB

Regardless of whether you decide on a homemade skylight, or a commercially-manufactured one, the first step is to install a *curb* for the skylight to sit on. The curb itself is made of 2″ × 6″ lumber that should be free from all but the tightest knots. Try to get pieces that aren't warped or bent. Pieces with cracks at the end (known as checked lumber) should also be discarded.

Figure 4 shows how to get the right curb measurement for the skylight you have decided to use.

Materials

To erect and install the curb completely, here is an alphabetical list of what you'll need:

1. *Aluminum flashing* — (obtainable in any hardware store) should be 9″ wide; it is sold by the foot.

2. Cement: you'll need two kinds:
   A. *Epoxy cement* — Any epoxy cement works, but PC-7, a two-part resin, is the one we used to seal the corners of the flashing.
   B. *Roof cement* comes in both one- and five-gallon quantities. You won't need five gallons, but it is cheaper to buy this way than the one-gallon can.

3. *Header material* should be the same size stock as the ceiling rafter.

4. *Nails:*
   A. *12-penny common nails* — used for nailing the curb together, the curb to roof sheathing, and the headers to rafters.
   B. *8-penny common nails,* used for nailing the curb to roof and bracing.
   C. *1″ galvanized roof nails,* for securing the roof material and for nailing the flashing to the top of the curb.

5. *2″ × 6″ material* — used for building the curb itself.

Always buy a little more supplies than you think you'll need. When it's ten P.M. Sunday, and you need *one* more tube of caulk, finding a place that's open is difficult, if not impossible. If you don't use your last tube of caulk, most stores will gladly give you a refund. Utility knife blades always seem to break at the least convenient times. Keep at least five spares in your toolbox, and you'll never be caught with your blades down.

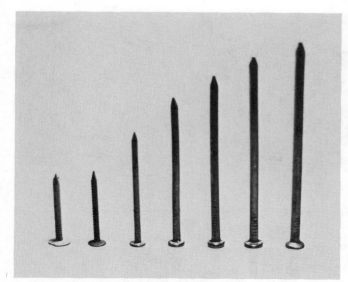

Nails for securing roofing material and drywall bear flat heads, and are shorter than nails used in frame construction.

Paying retail prices is not always necessary. Assemble your list of supplies and find a friendly contractor. Through his supply store, he can get you at least ten to fifteen percent off. Once you have the items on the list, you're ready to begin work.

MAKING THE CURB

When you are measuring and cutting, take your time and do it carefully. Try to remember this corny but true adage, "Measure twice, cut once." When you have the correct measurements, cut the pieces from your 2" × 6" material. Crooked cuts waste time and make you do the same work twice, but you can easily avoid this problem. When drawing measuring lines, use a felt-tipped pen (or a similar "no-mistake" marker) that gives you a thicker and more legible line than one drawn with a pencil.

A word of caution: Dull saw blades don't cut straight, require more effort to do a job, and can break. To make the job go faster and easier, have your saw(s) sharpened at a hardware store before you start work. When cutting, brace your body so that you can hold the saw firmly. Cutting properly takes time. Remember, quality, not speed, is your goal.

After the curb is nailed together, add the temporary corner braces to keep the curb square until it gets set on the roof. Make the

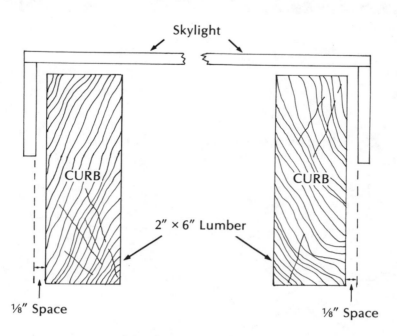

The external measurements of the curb should be ¼" less in both length and width than the internal length and width of the skylight.

FIGURE 4

Using a square ensures an accurate cut.

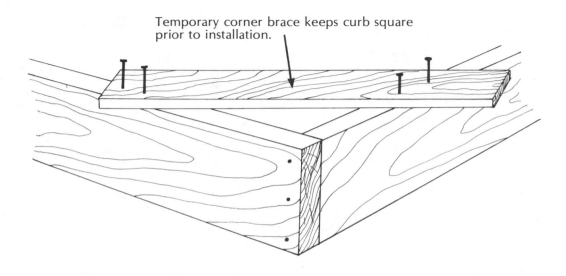

Temporary corner brace keeps curb square prior to installation.

FIGURE 5

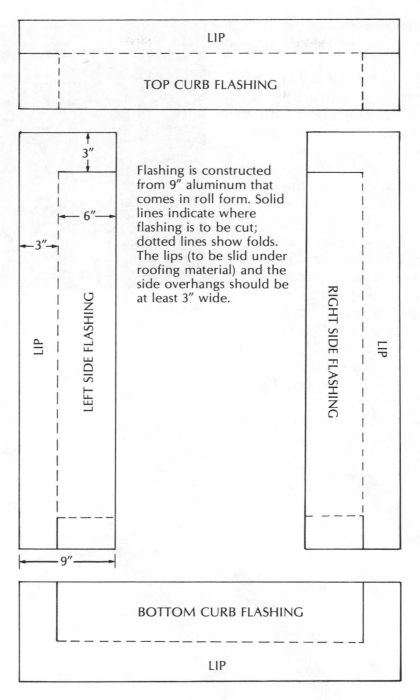

Flashing is constructed from 9" aluminum that comes in roll form. Solid lines indicate where flashing is to be cut; dotted lines show folds. The lips (to be slid under roofing material) and the side overhangs should be at least 3" wide.

FIGURE 6

braces out of scrap, and remove them after the curb is nailed in place. Use 6- or 8-penny common nails—but don't nail them in all the way, so you can pull them out easily (Figure 5).

Before you install the curb, apply the best quality sealer or polyurethane you can find. Once sealed, the wood will repel water over a long period of time, preventing contraction and expansion and decreasing the possibility of leaks.

ASSEMBLING THE FLASHING

Remember: in building a skylight, assembling the flashing is the most important step, since it determines whether your skylight is going to leak. Assemble the flashing around the curb *before* either the curb or the flashing is installed. (Your basement or garage is a good place to do this.)

To eliminate the chance of leakage, study the patterns in Figure 7. The overlap at each end of the flashing is three inches. The flap that slides under the roof is three inches also. No matter what size your skylight, you *always* need three inches of overlap at the corners, at least three inches of extension under the roofing material on *all* sides, and one inch of extension over the height of the curb, so that the flashing can be attached to the top of the curb.

In constructing a skylight, the important task is preparing the flashing correctly. A crooked cut on the flashing can be disastrous because your skylight will leak. The aluminum flashing (purchased at hardware stores or lumberyards) *can* be cut with a mat knife, or even a heavy pair of scissors. But use tin snips; they're easier to work with than a knife, and give a smoother cut on the edges.

Trying to bend flashing free-form style is

A completed curb, braced and ready for polyurethane.

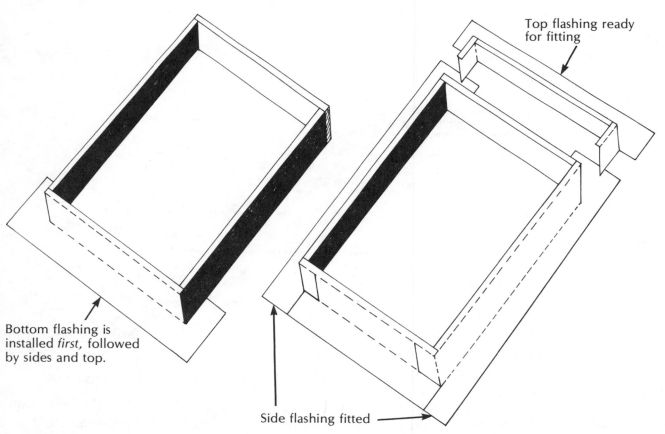

Top flashing ready for fitting

Bottom flashing is installed *first,* followed by sides and top.

Side flashing fitted

FIGURE 7

about as easy as trying to bend tissue paper. Rather than using the curb to help you form the flashing, use an unwarped two-by-four as an edge to bend the flashing over. This technique keeps the folds straight, which looks and fits better.

Even with diagrams to help you, cutting flashing can be tricky. Practice never hurt anybody. But since flashing is more expensive than paper, you can save money and frustration by constructing a full-size paper template for *each* piece of flashing diagrammed. If you have roofing tarpaper, use it; it's heavy enough to fold without being too cumbersome to work with. *Do not* make the aluminum pieces until you are certain that the paper templates are the right size!

Be sure everything fits *before* you lug it up to the roof and start applying cement. If you fail to do this and run into a problem on the roof *after* you've applied cement, you have a nasty problem because the cement has a cure time of about ½ hour. It may harden while you are cutting new flashing, which means you'll have to scrape out the cement and reapply—a filthy and time-consuming job.

5 Installing the Flashing and Curb

*I*n most instances, skylight installation is best tackled by more than one person. An assistant can be invaluable, especially when helping with the tactical work such as measuring and cutting. Having someone else on the job allows a point of view you may not have been aware of. Even someone who just handles the mundane chores like getting supplies or making coffee can save tremendous amounts of time.

CHOOSING A CREW

Here are some suggestions for picking a crew who'll help make your project go as smoothly as possible:

- *Do* get someone who is reliable and willing to work. Having a master carpenter as an assistant does you no good if that person doesn't show up or won't cooperate.
- *Do* stay away from well-meaning but inept friends. The wrong choice for a partner can detract from what should be an enjoyable experience.
- *Don't* assemble a committee. That old saying about too many cooks spoiling the soup is absolutely true. The worst handicap is a group standing around making off-the-cuff suggestions, but contributing nothing. I've seen too many mistakes made and too much time wasted by these "experts" barking out orders as if they were the pharaohs in charge of constructing the pyramids. Limit your helpers to one or two at most.
- *Do* find someone whose work skills and habits are compatible with yours. Many of my autumn weekends are spent in the woods felling and chopping trees. The work can be dangerous: one slip of the chainsaw could be fatal. The only person I trust with me is my father. We've worked together for years and have developed an understanding of what the other is doing. We get more done in a few minutes than most teams can do in an hour. Most importantly, we do it *safely*; neither of us has ever been injured cutting down trees.

   Naturally, putting in a skylight is a lot safer than running a chainsaw, but a sloppy or careless aide can endanger you. A simple rule of thumb: anybody who disregards his or her own safety isn't likely to look out for *your* welfare. Avoid these types.
- *Do* find a helper who will follow your instructions. You've invested considerable amounts of time, money, and preparation in this project: you're the boss. If your helper balks at doing things your way, he shouldn't be there. It is one thing for your helper to offer a suggestion, but unless he or she has vast amounts of experience, assume your way is the right way.

Even prefab skylights (such as this model by APC Corporation) are installed faster with one team member inside the house to pass up tools and supplies.

SAFETY TIPS—BEFORE STARTING WORK

First of all: get rid of bugs. Bees and wasps frequently nest in attics and under eaves. One or two days before you build your skylight, spray under the roof with a pesticide recommended by your hardware store. You won't have insects to contend with, nor will the pesticides bother you during building if you spray beforehand.

Broken rungs, rotted wood, and slippery footing on a wooden ladder are not just annoying, but dangerous as well. Aluminum ladders are a better choice. They won't break or wear out—and make a better long-term investment. Anchor your ladder firmly to the ground. Don't lean it against gutters, which aren't designed to support that much weight and may collapse if too much pressure is applied.

Block off the ground below your work area—on *both* sides of the house. Occasionally, scrap or stray objects fall from the roof, so to avoid injury or damage, cordon off the area with ropes or long boards. Make a sign out of cardboard or scrap plywood to warn people below to keep their distance. If the roof you'll be working on is anywhere near your driveway, MOVE YOUR CAR TO THE STREET! Even a truck doesn't hold up well when scraps fall on it.

Tell spectators politely but firmly to find more interesting pursuits. Hangers-on are a nuisance: they distract you, waste your time, and get in your way.

UP ON THE ROOF—AGAIN

Remember, the fewer tools you have to lug up there, the better off you'll be. If you can cut, drill, or sand in your basement or workshop, do so. It's much easier than doing it up in the attic.

I once witnessed a man cut through his own power saw extension cord! Fortunately, he was not electrocuted, though he might well have been. The saddest part of on-the-job accidents is that most result through carelessness, and that an alarmingly high percentage of them could have been prevented. No amount of insurance money can compensate for the loss suffered by serious injury. But don't be intimidated by skylight installation. It's not particularly dangerous if you take proper precautions.

Have a first-aid kit handy. Serious injuries are rare among roofers, but skinned knuckles, small knife cuts, and asphalt burns are all too common. To keep a minor cut from becoming infected, use an antiseptic such as Merthiolate and a clean, fresh Band-Aid.

Place roof cement where it can't tip over or roll away.

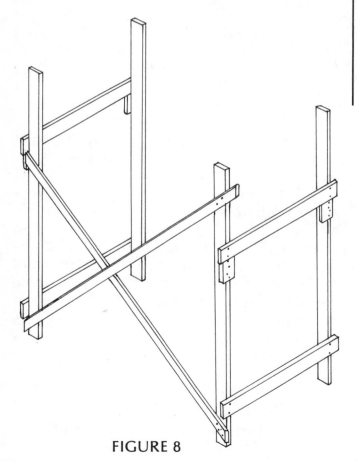

This scaffold should be used when there's no other place to erect a work platform. (If the work height is over 8 feet, rent a commercial scaffold for greater safety.)

Use 2" × 4"s for uprights and crossmembers, fastened with common 12-penny nails. For the diagonal bracing, use 1" × 3" firring strips; for longer lengths, overlap two pieces by 12". (Be sure to brace horizontally as well.)

FIGURE 8

Also, for less than five dollars, you can get a nail-holding apron and hammer holder to slip on your belt. The apron keeps the nails off the roof, where they can puncture a shingle or help your foot slip. The holder keeps the hammer handy and keeps *it* from falling off the roof. The first day I ever worked on a roof, I didn't have one of these, and my hammer slid off the roof seven times.

If you're carrying heavy and/or bulky objects on a roof, your weight distribution changes drastically. Large objects (plywood sheets are the most notorious) get blown around in the wind all too easily. Heavy objects like a bale of shingles make your balance awkward. Practice by walking around on the ground with any big object *before* you try to walk around with one on the roof.

Take your tool box on the roof with you and set it down nearby. Then forget your worries about misplacing tools, tools falling off, and stepping on hammers. Also, take an old coffee can or jar with you for old nails or screws. This keeps them in one place, and avoids their rolling around or getting stepped on.

If you have the choice, work inside the attic, where you'll have a level surface to stand on. When working on rafters, tack down one or more sheets of plywood with 8-penny nails. That will give you a stable area to work on without having to worry about balancing on beams. Don't stand on potentially dangerous old chairs or tables. If you're perched precariously on a

rickety structure, you'll spend all your time concentrating on just maintaining your balance, and you'll be distracted from the task at hand: putting in a skylight. Instead, use a scaffold, which makes the job much easier anytime you have to go over ten feet high. Either construct one as shown (Figure 8) or take advantage of the relatively inexpensive rental rates.

CUTTING THE HOLE IN YOUR ROOF

After you draw the outside roofline for your skylight, place the curb on it. Look at it from ground level. Does it look straight? I put a skylight in an old mansion with a badly warped roof. What *looked* straight and what *measured* straight were completely different. Let your eyes judge. If it looks good, then install it that

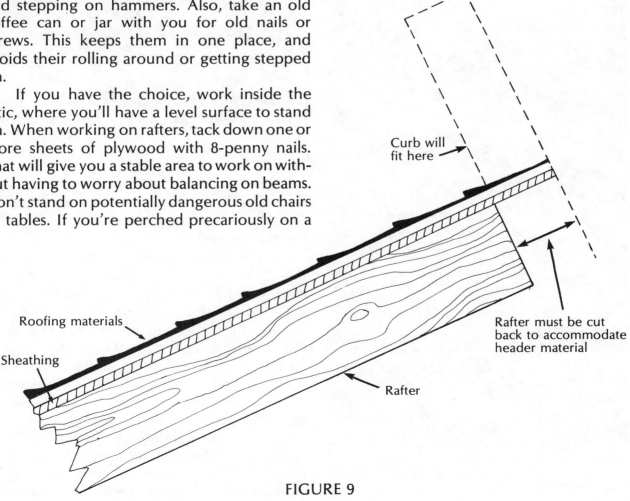

Curb will fit here

Rafter must be cut back to accommodate header material

Roofing materials

Sheathing

Rafter

FIGURE 9

From inside, cut back rafters, as shown in Figure 9.

With utility knife or chisel, cut back the roofing material.

Trace a line around the curb, showing where the roofing material is to be cut back (courtesy APC Corporation).

way. Check the measurements: the opening should have the same dimensions as the curb's internal measurements.

Unsure as to the *exact* size needed? Make the cut a little smaller than necessary. You can always enlarge the hole, but if you cut one too large, you'll have problems. The first skylight I put in, the roof hole was cut too big. But it didn't cause any permanent problems, because we used oversized flashing on the outside; and on the inside, we put double two-by-sixes on the sides. The finished result looked like it had been designed that way on purpose.

In less temperate climates, loss of hot or cold air from the inside of the house can pose a problem. It's best prevented by finishing all the work on the roof *before* you cut the hole in the ceiling. This way you retain the benefit of attic insulation, and there's another big advantage as well: by completing and sealing off the outside work first, you can build and decorate the shaftway at your leisure.

After checking the measurements, cut through the rafters, allowing 1⅝" on each side to allow for the nailing of the headers, as in Figure 9. Do not cut into the sheathing just yet —cut and remove the rafters only. But never, *ever* throw things off the roof without looking first. Last summer, some moron in my crew hurled a four-foot section of a two-by-four (complete with eight rusty nails) off a 40-foot roof—and missed me by less than 12 inches.

One way to cut the sheathing and roofing material is to do it from the inside. This eliminates some of the climbing on the roof. To cut the skylight from the inside, just set your power

saw to the thickness of the sheathing and cut along the line you laid out before. But be careful. A power saw turned loose can slice off your fingers in a heartbeat.

To avoid slipping, always brace your feet firmly. This also gives you sufficient leverage to cut a straight line. Use safety goggles—particularly when you're using power tools. They're cheap, don't obstruct your view as much as glasses, and prevent wood chips or nails from landing in your eyes.

Understandably, you may be reluctant to attempt cutting with the power saw above your head. It's difficult for anyone, perhaps even foolhardy for a beginner. But there is an easier way. Drive a nail through the roof at each corner of the opening to be cut. Then go up on the roof with the curb, power saw, flooring chisels, hammer, and chalk line. If you have a

With a power saw, cut through the sheathing. Notice how the workman stays low and braced on the roof, to avoid crooked cuts and potential accidents (courtesy APC Corporation)!

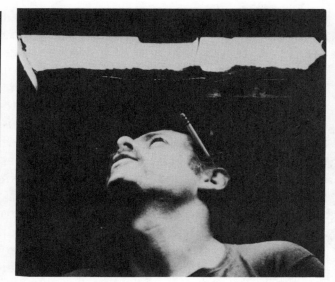

The roof is now open.

Trim back roofing material to allow for curb installation.

Cut tin (if any) and pry back.

Sheathing is now completely exposed.

tin roof, take the tin snips too. When you locate the four corners, take the curb and put it over the four corner nails. Trace a line around the *outside* of the curb, indicating how far the roof material is to be cut back.

After cutting the sheathing, cut the roofing material with a mat knife (for shingle roofs) or a flooring chisel (for tin or composite roofs). Beginners often remove too many shingles. When you cut the roofing material around the perimeter of the curb, make certain that you cut *completely* through each shingle. This prevents you from inadvertently ripping out adjacent shingles, and gives you a straight line to work with.

After the roofing material is cleared away, lay the curb back down on the now-bare sheathing and trace a line around the *inside* of the curb. Before cutting, make sure your extension cords are in top condition. Now is not the time to get knocked off the roof by a shorted-out cord. To open the roof, remove the curb and cut along the line you have drawn. Pay attention; power tools can be dangerous.

After cutting, clean up the area. Check especially for loose nails, frequently the culprits responsible for a slip. After you are done cleaning up, take a break—your helpers won't mind a bit.

SETTING THE FLASHING

If you're working with someone else, one of you should stay outside on the roof, the other inside. It's much easier to pass tools, glue, etc., through that hole in the ceiling, than to make constant treks up and down the ladder.

Make sure the roof material is free from sheathing for at least four inches around. Also remove any nails that might stop you from sliding the flashing in. See the drawing in Figure 10.

Take the curb and flashing up on the roof with your five gallons of roof cement, old gloves, paint thinner, and a bunch of rags (this job has a tendency to get a little messy).

Even if you were satisfied with your basement trial-fit, do another fitting on the roof just to be on the safe side. If the flashing and curb fit correctly in the basement *and* on the roof, *then* you can apply the cement. To keep the mess down, coat only one side of the skylight at a

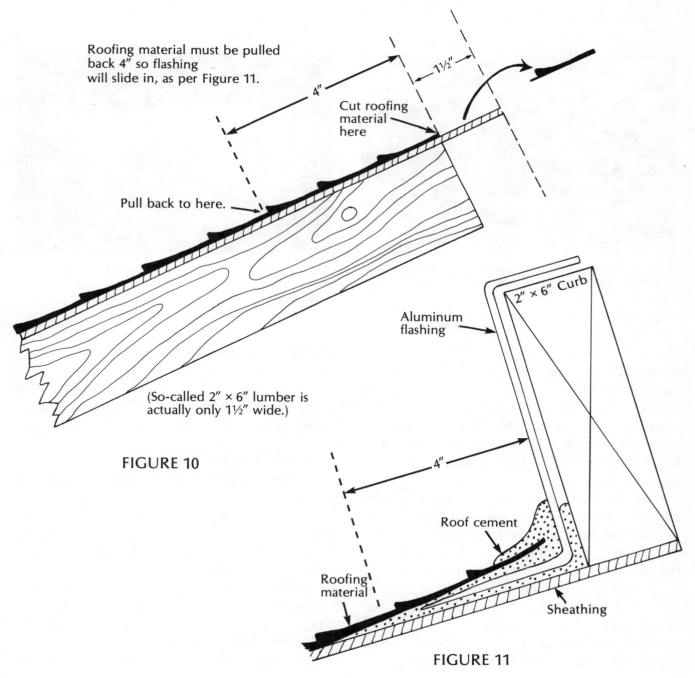

Roofing material must be pulled back 4" so flashing will slide in, as per Figure 11.

4"

1½"

Cut roofing material here

Pull back to here.

(So-called 2" × 6" lumber is actually only 1½" wide.)

FIGURE 10

2" × 6" Curb

Aluminum flashing

4"

Roof cement

Roofing material

Sheathing

FIGURE 11

1. Pry up roofing material so that flashing can be inserted.

2. Apply layer of roofing cement to sheathing before inserting flashing. (Note bottom side of flashing, already in place.)

3. Toenail the curb to existing rafters.

4. The completed curb, seen from below.

time. Don't want to get your hands sticky when you apply the roof cement? An old plastic spatula or frosting knife is the answer. Dip the spatula in the roofing cement and use it like a spoon to apply the cement. Then feather out the edges with the spatula for an even finish. The end result looks more professional and is easier to clean up.

Pay close attention to your flashing's fitting and cementing, and save yourself the aggravation of having to go back and figure out where that drip is coming from. Always put on a little more roof cement than necessary; any excess can be removed after a day or two. At worst, too much cement is a little messy, but not enough can cause leaks.

After you put down a good layer of roof cement, slide the bottom piece of flashing un-der the roof incline. Next, apply another coat of cement, and do the left and right sides.

Put in the top last (Figure 7). Bind back all the flashings so they will not get in the way of setting in the curb—which is your next step.

INSTALLING THE CURB

The curb should sit down on the sheathing and be nailed around the sheathing's edge with 12-penny common nails (Figure 12). When hammering in nails, hold the hammer towards the bottom of the handle. Bend your wrist, not your forearm. Pounding in nails with your forearms will quickly wear you out. Flick your wrist as though you were drinking a shot of whisky, allowing the natural momentum of the hammer's head to do most of the work.

When driving nails through the roof, make

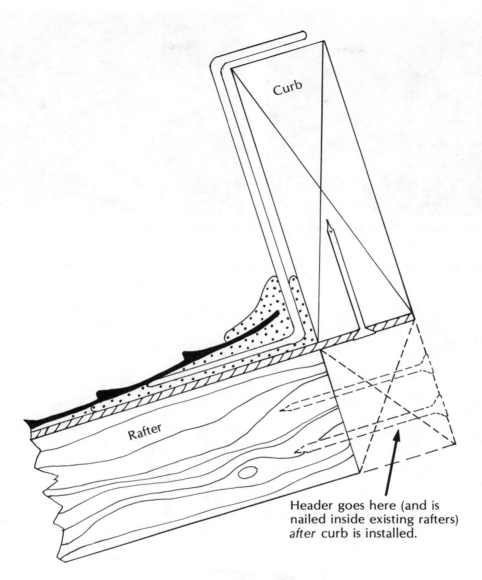

Header goes here (and is nailed inside existing rafters) *after* curb is installed.

FIGURE 12

certain they go in straight. A simple way to check this is with the level. If the angle is the same on all four nails, they are straight. If not, remove the "odd" crooked nail and try again. If any nails get bent while being hammered in, daub the replacement nail with silicone caulk as double insurance against leaks from a too-big hole.

Toenail any rafters to the curb with 8-penny common nails (Figure 13), and counter-sink or punch in the nails so that the heads are not visible. Cover the whole with Plastic Wood, and it won't be noticeable from below.

Next, bend up the flashing. But before you nail the flashing to the *top* of the curb, make sure the curb is even. Plane out any high spots, and double-check with your level. Pre-drill all nail holes with a 1/16" drill bit: this keeps the wood from splitting. Coat the nails with a heavy layer of caulk to help seal the holes.

Some pre-fab skylights, like this Wasco model, have their own built-in curbs. If so, simply nail down the roofing material before dropping the skylight into place.

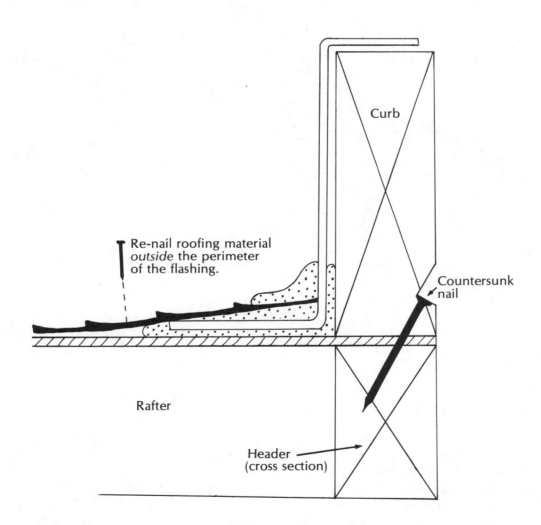

Curb

Re-nail roofing material *outside* the perimeter of the flashing.

Countersunk nail

Rafter

Header (cross section)

FIGURE 13

Space one-inch galvanized nails 3½" apart and nail the top of the flashing to the curb. *Remember, if you are making a plate-style skylight, you must nail a batten over the flashing.* If you try to drive a nail into another nail, you could split one of the curb's sides, ruining everything you've worked so hard to accomplish. So space the *flashing* nails 3½" apart now, and the *batten* nails 4" apart.

Cover the corners with a coat of epoxy (PC-7 is excellent here), following the directions on the can. Cover the edge of the roof material with a coat of roof cement as in Figure 13. Clean up the area, your tools, and yourself —and that just about does it for installing the curb.

The only thing left to do is to nail the roof material back in place. First, dip your nails in roofing cement. This may be messy, but it will reduce leaks. Next, drive in the nails, making sure not to put any nails into the flashing itself. Then nail in the headers (which should be the same material as the rafters) with 12-penny nails. This finishes the installation of the curb.

6 Finishing the Plexiglas or Plate Glass Skylight

Many kinds of transparent and translucent materials can be put on the curb. For the home skylight builder, Plexiglas or plate glass seem to work very well. (But only high-quality craftsmanship will avoid leakage for *any* type of skylight.)

Among skylights, the Plexiglas or plate glass type is probably the most common and one of the easier skylights to build—for good reasons. The materials are standard and easy to obtain, and the construction methods simple enough for the weekend carpenter. But the biggest advantage is the large variety of materials that can be laid along the top edge of the curb. Clear, tinted, or translucent white Plexiglas (which allows light, but not images, to pass through it) can all be used. (Figure 15 shows all the components assembled.)

If you don't want to prune your overhanging trees, construct a screen guard (described in Chapter 14), or find a new location for your skylight. If you need the safety of a high-strength material, consider wire-glass, which can be purchased at any good glass store (consult your local Yellow Pages). You could even install tempered, bullet-proof glass. The grade-8 strength variety will protect the skylight from flammable liquids and any gunfire below .50 caliber. But the expense isn't justified if your vandalism problems are limited to kids with B-B guns.

After erecting the curb, check to see if all the top edges of the curb are even. If not, sand or plane them flush. The next step is to nail a spacer, called a batten, around the outside edge of the curb. This will hold the aluminum angle at the proper space above the plate to allow for the silicone caulk. The batten strip should be about ½" to ¾" wide, depending on the size of the skylight material. The gap between the batten and the material should be twice as thick as the Plexiglas you're using. If your material is plate glass, a gap of ⅛" is sufficient. Nail the batten around the edge with 4-penny finish nails.

THE ALUMINUM ANGLE

The next step is to prepare the aluminum angle, used to hold down the Plexiglas or plate glass with the aid of the silicone caulk. Your aluminum angle should be 3" × 3" wide. Cut it to size by using your curb's dimensions for your measurements. For the woodscrew and gasket assembly to fit tightly, you've got to drill holes in the aluminum. Doing this ahead of time makes the job go much easier. Also, countersink the holes as in Figure 14 to allow for the faucet washer gasket.

Screw the aluminum angle on top of the flashing *and* the batten. Space these screws at 5" intervals, to avoid the nails in the curb and batten. Also, use 2" #8 wood screws, instead of the 1" screws you use on the sides, because you have to go through an extra ¾" of wood.

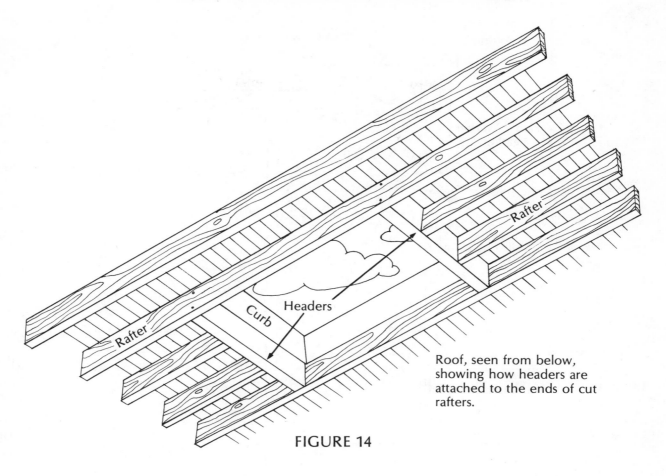

Headers

Curb

Rafter

Rafter

Roof, seen from below, showing how headers are attached to the ends of cut rafters.

FIGURE 14

Space the holes on the sides 9" apart (not 5" apart, as on top), and you won't have to worry about nails and screws meeting each other. The screw holes on the *sides* of the aluminum angle should be ½" from the bottom of the angle; those on top should be centered on the batten's middle. As you should know by now, the best way to do this is to trial fit, mark, and measure the aluminum angle *before* it gets put on.

Install the aluminum angle with the *side pieces over the top and bottom ones*. This will give your skylight a natural run-off, which keeps water from accumulating on the skylight's base, where it could eventually develop into a leak.

Cut the batten to size.

Nail a batten atop the curb.

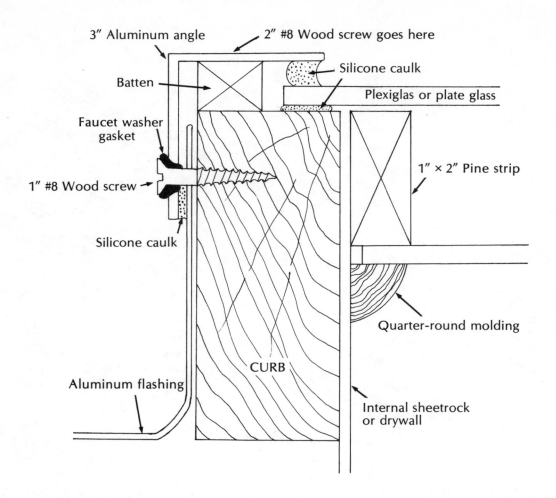

FIGURE 15

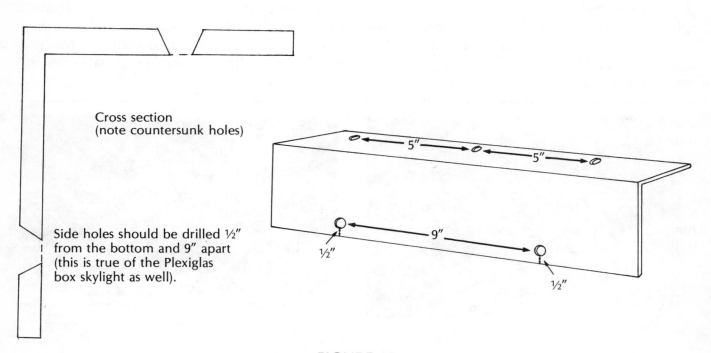

FIGURE 16

Measure the completed curb to determine the length of the aluminum angle.

Mark the aluminum angle for cutting.

Lay the first line of caulk atop the batten.

Caulk comes in both tubes and cartridges. Buy both. You will use the cartridge for caulking the top of the skylight, where a wide bead (layer of caulk) is required. The tube will be used for tight spots, such as under the aluminum angle on the sides of the skylight. Cut the cartridge tip ¼" wide. Cut the tube tip ⅛" for a finer bead. Check the cure time on your caulk and roof cement. Most are about a half-hour, which means you must do any repairs or adjustments within that time, before your adhesives become almost impossible to work with.

APPLYING THE PLEXIGLAS (OR PLATE GLASS)

When you have the aluminum angle prepared, the batten nailed in place, and the curb ready to receive the skylight material, lay a bead of silicone caulk around the curb or ½" from the inside edge of the curb. When you cut the top off the caulk tube, don't cut a hole over ⁵⁄₁₆" wide; ¼" is the best. After the caulk is laid out, peel one side of the protective paper off the material. A little trick: if you are handling a large sheet of Plexiglas, lay some thin pieces of wood across the skylight so they rest on the battens. Then you can lay the sheet on these and position it before setting it in place.

Once the Plexiglas is evenly spaced between the battens and you're ready to set it in place, just slide out the wooden strips one by one. Let the skylight material settle onto the silicone caulk on the curb and press it into place. Then remove the paper from the remaining side and lay down another bead of caulk on the skylight material. Make sure the bead of caulk is *higher* than the batten, so that when you set down the aluminum angle, it will meet the silicone to form the seal.

Don't try to force stubborn screws into place, or you may crack the wood. Instead, rub the threads on a bar of hand soap and they'll slide into place. After doing that, remove them, coat with caulk, and reinsert.

CAULKING

After the aluminum is set and screwed into place, coat all seams of the aluminum angle with a layer of silicone caulk. Remember that spatula you used to feather out the roofing cement? The same technique works with caulk,

2. *Screw the aluminum angle to the curb.*

1. *Install aluminum angle over the plate glass or Plexiglas.*

3. *Close-up of screw and washer in place.*

4. *A third and final bead of caulk goes between aluminum angle and the top surface of the skylight material.*

Caulking is messy, so have plenty of paper towels handy to wipe up the excess. Don't use turpentine or industrial solvents, which can dull Plexiglas. If the caulk won't wipe up with paper towels, use a rag with a *very* small amount of floor wax remover. Don't use too much, or it will soak into your caulking, making it impossible to cure.

If a friend helped you do a professional job installing your skylight, don't forget to show your gratitude—this final point is nothing more than good manners. Your sincere thanks for a job well done probably means as much as any wages you might pay. If your associates did a good job, tell them!

Clean up the scrap and loose nails, then you're ready to go down and enjoy your skylight. But go back on the roof and double-check the caulking in forty-eight hours (ample time for these substances to cure permanently, and for any cracks or potential leaks to show up).

except use a wooden dowel or length of old broom handle instead of the spatula. The result: a professional-looking, semi-circular bead. Cover all exposed screw heads with silicone as well. Check the flashing and the roof material, and coat any problems with a layer of roof cement.

7 Finishing the Plexiglas Box Skylight

The box-frame skylight (as shown in Figure 17) offers another solution to the problem of making the joint between the skylight and the curb watertight. This type of skylight is built to fit over the top of the curb; its sides extend down over the curb's exterior sides, eliminating the need for the top flashing, the batten strip around the edge of the curb, and the aluminum angle. In solving this problem, however, most of us have to learn a whole new skill: cutting and cementing Plexiglas.

If you are going to build this kind of skylight, read very carefully the following section on "Tips on Working with Plexiglas." Also, pick up a booklet called "Do it Yourself with Plexiglas" from your Plexiglas dealer. You may even find it easier to make a box-frame than to work with aluminum angle.

To get proper measurements for the box skylight and to allow for the expansion and contraction of the Plexiglas, you must measure the length and width of the curb. To these measurements, add ¼" for each 4' of skylight material and add ½" for the two sides (¼" per side). These new measurements are for the top of the box skylight. Next you will need four 4" strips for the sides.

After cutting these 4" strips to the proper length, drill the holes for the hold-down screws. Countersink the holes to allow for the faucet washer gasket. These holes should be about 2" in from the end, about 1½" from the bottom, and spaced about 12" on center (that is, 12" from the center of one hole to the center of the next). When you drill the holes, use a block of wood to back up the work to minimize the chance of the plastic cracking. Once the holes are drilled, glue the side strips to the skylight top.

TIPS ON WORKING WITH PLEXIGLAS

Cutting, drilling, and gluing Plexiglas for the box-style skylight aren't hard—they just take a little getting used to. When cutting the ¼" Plexiglas, use a blade with 14 teeth per inch. To cut a straight line, clamp a straightedge to the sheet as a guide. Do the same for circular hand saws. For circular hand and table saws, use the type of crosscut blade recommended for finish cuts on veneer plywood.

Remember to hold the material firmly as you cut and not to forcefeed it either. Also, don't remove the paper backing when you cut Plexiglas. (You can save your scraps and make a mobile. Simply cut the pieces to the desired shape and string them up with monofilament fishing line attached with epoxy glue.)

When *drilling* Plexiglas, always back up the material with a block of wood. Make sure the drill bit is sharp. With an electric drill, I recommend Hanson's Special Purpose High Speed

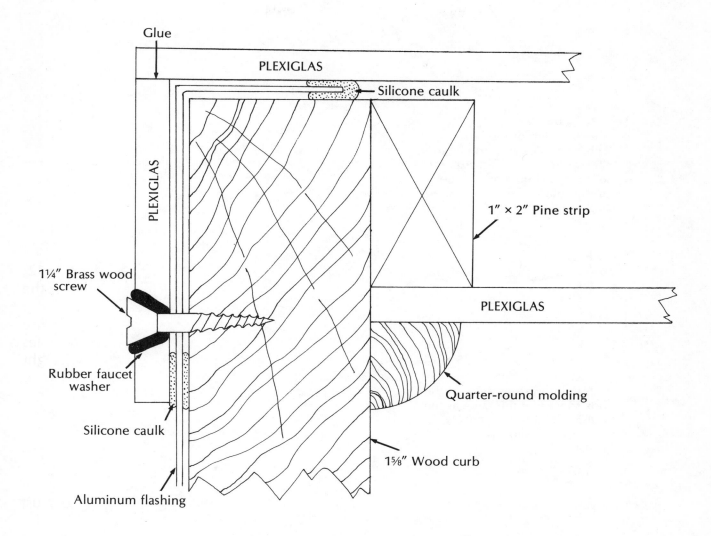

FIGURE 17

Bits, but any good sharp bit will do if you are very careful. For small holes like the ones for the screw and faucet washer gasket, highest speed is best. When your bit is about to come through the far side, slow down to avoid chipping. After the hole is drilled, go back with your screw, and set and countersink for the faucet washer.

When drilling holes in the side of the Plexiglas box, allow for the expansion and contraction of the Plexiglas. A rule of thumb: drill holes 1/16" oversize for every foot on the side. Keep at

least 1/4" of material from the circumference of the drill hole to the edge of the piece.

While there are various ways to finish the edges for the sake of appearance, your main concern is to *prepare the edge for gluing.* To do this, first scrape the edge with the back of a hacksaw blade or sand it down with 80-grit production paper. After the saw marks are gone, change over to 150-grit wet or dry paper to give you a clean satin finish. Be sure *not* to round the edges while sanding. Now you are ready to start gluing.

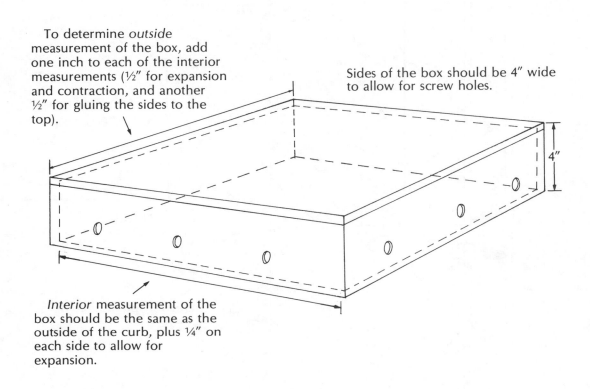

To determine *outside* measurement of the box, add one inch to each of the interior measurements (½″ for expansion and contraction, and another ½″ for gluing the sides to the top).

Sides of the box should be 4″ wide to allow for screw holes.

4″

Interior measurement of the box should be the same as the outside of the curb, plus ¼″ on each side to allow for expansion.

FIGURE 18

While drilling, place a board beneath the Plexiglas to prevent chipping.

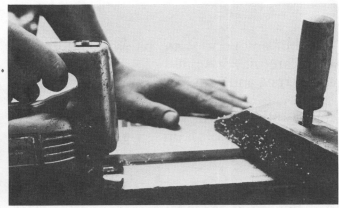

When cutting Plexiglas, use a straight piece of lumber as a guide.

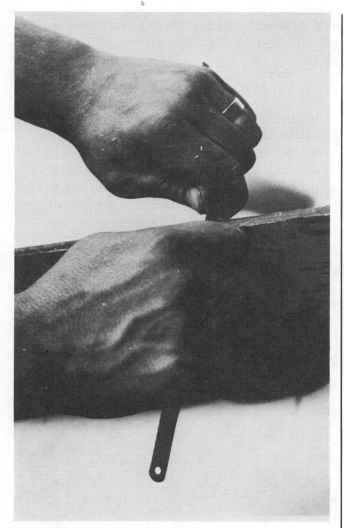

Scrape the Plexiglas with the back of a hacksaw blade to ensure a good glue joint.

Tape the pieces of the Plexiglas box before gluing.

There are two types of cement for Plexiglas: capillary cement and thickened cement. You should use both types with great care, and avoid the vapors as much as possible. Capillary cement can only be used with Plexiglas G (general purpose). After the edge has been sanded satin-smooth, pull the paper back slightly and tape two pieces together with masking tape. Apply the capillary cement with a needle (an applicator you can purchase from the place where you got the acrylic sheet). Keep the joint horizontal to allow the cement to flow properly.

Thickened cement is applied differently. After checking for a proper fit, apply a small bead of cement to one piece, then join the two pieces together and clamp until set.

After the skylight box frame is made, lay a bead of silicone caulk around the top edge of the curb and set the Plexiglas box over it. Wiggle it slightly to help spread the caulk. Fasten the box to the curb by installing wood screws and faucet washers (as a gasket) through the sides of the Plexiglas box and into the side of the curb. Pull off the remaining paper backing and enjoy the new-found light.

CHECKING FOR LEAKS

Once your skylight is installed, check it for leaks before you leave the job site. An excellent way to water-test your workmanship is to bring a hose up to the roof. (If you have a problem getting water onto the roof, wait until it rains.) Do this testing *before* building the shaft.

A word of warning: water makes the roof very slippery and hard to walk on. Arrange the test so that you will not have to walk over any area which has been wet down with the hose. Then douse the whole skylight with water. Also wet down the area around the skylight. Where the aluminum flashing slides under the roof covering material is where most leaks develop. Have a helper inside the attic spot for leaks.

If you find a leak in the flashing area, first check to see if any of the roofing nails securing the roof covering have punctured the new flashing. To fix this kind of leak, remove the nail and cover the hole with roof cement.

If no nails seem to be puncturing the flashing, then the leak problem is due to insufficient coating of roof cement on the roof surface. With additional cement, recoat the whole area where the flashing meets the roof material.

The only other area where a leak may develop is where the Plexiglas is joined to the curb. Check under the aluminum angle. Is there enough silicone caulk between the sky-light material and the aluminum flashing? Pay special attention to the corners where the aluminum angles meet.

A FINAL WORD ON QUALITY

Following these steps to the letter assures you of a job to be proud of for a long time. None of them involve extraordinary skill, just methodical execution. Now that you have successfully built your skylight, read on—and discover how to make the inside as professional as the outside.

This expanded shaftway enhances the size of a Lynbrook Glass skylight.

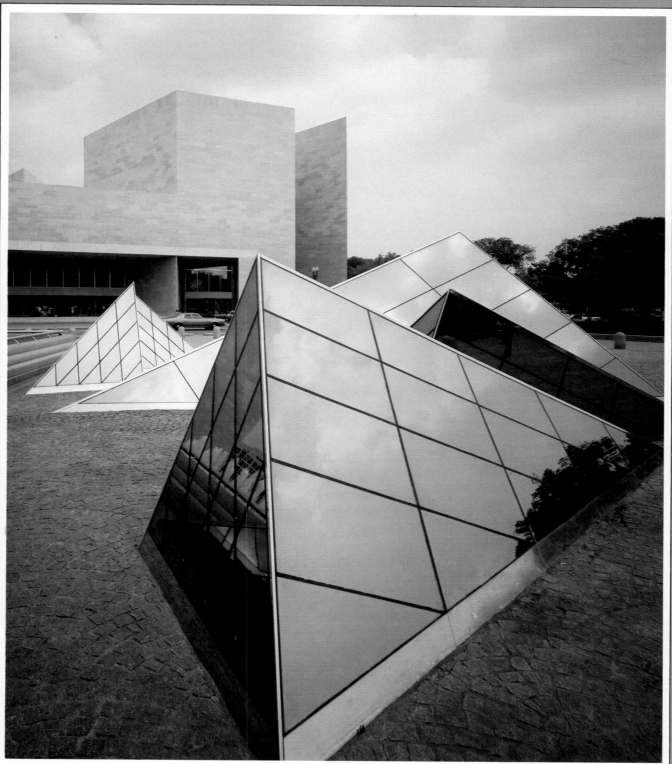

Plate 1. *Mirrored pyramidal skylights in the National Gallery of Art Plaza, Washington, D.C.* (Photo courtesy Super Sky Products, Inc.)

Plate 2. *Standard dome sky-light brightens an indoor swimming pool in Detroit.* (Super Sky Products, Inc.)

Plate 3. *Multiple pyramidal skylights take a Houston swimming pool to the outdoors.* (Super Sky Products, Inc.)

Plate 4. *Low-profile sloped glazing system matches sliding glass doors—and permits solar heating.* (Wasco Products, Inc.)

Plate 5. *Vault skylights—with variable rafter segmentation—give a complete view of the heavens.* (Super Sky Products, Inc.)

Plate 6. *First step in opening your ceiling: measure and mark the location —ideally, between rafters.*

Plate 7. *Cut along marks, supporting the ceiling to prevent cracking.*

Plate 9. *Finish drywall, let dry, and paint to match ceiling.* (All photos: Wasco Products, Inc.)

Plate 8. *Frame the shaftway with drywall, nailed to ceiling joists and headers.*

Plate 11. *Venting Skywindow features a built-in curb with fiberglass insulation.* (Wasco Products, Inc.)

Plate 10. *Exterior view of the sloped glazing system in Plate 4.* (Wasco Products, Inc.)

Plate 12. *Double-domed Cellar Garden Bubble directs natural light into the basement.* (Dilworth Manufacturing Co.)

Plate 13. *Apex of pyramidal skylight can be modified to hold light fixtures or ventilation fans.* (Super Sky Products, Inc.)

Plate 14. *Narrow hallway brightened by skylights, center, and recessed lighting, along brick wall.* (Rainbow Manufacturing)

Plate 15. *A splayed shaftway, with its ceiling opening larger than the roof opening, helps spread daylight.* (Wasco Products, Inc.)

Plate 18. *Stargazers are pre-assembled skylights with 1″ insulated safety glass. Note tracked blinds for blocking sunlight.* (Imperial Glass Structures Co.)

Plate 16. *Flat skylight, lying as close as possible to the roof to admit the most light.* (Bristol Fiberlite Industries)

Plate 17. *Dayliter Long-Lites install between rafters, so no cutting is necessary.* (APC Corporation)

Plate 19. *Decahedronal dome skylight brightens a fountain in Chicago's Ritz Carlton Hotel.* (Super Sky Products, Inc.)

Plate 20. Custom-designed skylights on the roof of World of Birds at New York's Bronx Zoo. (Fisher Skylights, Inc.)

Plate 21. *Barrel skylight system protects the walkway between two Bell Telephone buildings.*

Plate 22. *Clusters of acrylic bubbles replace sections of flat roof.* (Both photos: Naturalite, Inc.)

Plate 23. *Exterior view of the Dayliter Long-Lites in Plate 17.* (APC Corporation)

Plate 24. *Skywindow bubble designed especially to fit over thick wooden shingles or Spanish tile.* (Wasco Products, Inc.)

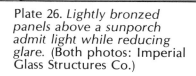

Plate 25. *Exterior view of the Stargazer panels in Plate 18.*

Plate 26. *Lightly bronzed panels above a sunporch admit light while reducing glare.* (Both photos: Imperial Glass Structures Co.)

Plate 27. *Helicopter lofts a custom-made skylight during construction of World Trade Center, Dallas.* (Fisher Skylights, Inc.)

Plate 28. *Tubular aluminum-framed skylight in Memphis's Commercial and Industrial Bank.* (Both photos: Fisher Skylights, Inc.)

Plate 29. *Continuous vaulted skylight in solar bronze finish allows only 50% light transmission.* (Naturalite, Inc.)

Plate 30. *Polygonal skylight in an Indiana shopping mall is equipped with floodlights for night-time illumination.* (Imperial Glass Structures Co.)

Plate 31. *Single-Slope skylights in a Chicago condominium.* (Both photos: Super Sky Products, Inc.)

Plate 32. *Custom-made bronzed skylights aligned vertically, like the prow of a ship, at a California cemetery.*

Plate 33. *Polygonal dome combined with vertical panels at Super Sky Products's offices, Mequon, Wisconsin.* (Super Sky Products, Inc.)

Plate 34. *Ridge Module skylights, designed to straddle the roof's very peak.* (Bristol Fiberlite Industries)

Plate 35. *Continuous module skylight extends the length of a narrow hall.* (Bristol Fiberlite Industries)

Plate 36. *Skylights arranged into geodesic domes for Milwaukee's Mitchell Park Conservatory.* (Super Sky Products, Inc.)

8 Constructing the Shaftway

*I*f your skylight was built in a roof that also functions as a ceiling, you don't need to be concerned about framing in anything; there will be no shaftway. But if your skylight is set in a roof which is *not* the ceiling, then your construction requires a shaft between roof and ceiling. You will have to cut a hole in the ceiling and the inside of this opening will have to be framed in, like the one that you cut in the roof. But first, decide what shape you want your shaftway to be.

Here, your options are limited only by the length and width of your ceiling. If you want the ceiling opening to be the same size as your skylight, drop a plumb line from the center of each corner where the rafters and headers intersect. Make certain that cuts running along the ceiling joists are *inside* the joists. This way, the joists provide a nailing surface for the shaftway covering—which in turn will hide the joists.

Before you cut the hole in the ceiling, remove all insulation from that section. This will prevent messy insulation from falling on the floor below, and avoid the possibility of your saw blade getting tangled in the insulation. Insulation, particularly the asbestos-type found in older houses, can pose a significant health hazard. To avoid breathing hazardous particles, wear an O.S.H.A.-approved mask. (Your hardware dealer will recommend the correct one.)

Spread an old sheet, shower curtain, or tablecloth on the floor beneath where you're working. It will catch the sawdust and insulation scraps that fall, saving you the trouble of sweeping or vacuuming them up. Once you have cut the hole in the ceiling, you are ready to begin building the small walls that will form a shaft from the roof skylight to the ceiling opening.

FRAMING

The materials for framing the shaft walls should be 2" × 3" studs. The frame will help stabilize the construction of the skylight and will serve as nail blocks for the shaft wall covering and any electrical boxes (see following chapter).

The stud wall should be flush with the ceiling header and should be set back from the roof header by the thickness of the wall covering. (See Figure 20). Notice there are two types of walls. If your roof has no pitch, you will need only the first type of wall—one that runs perpendicular to the roof and ceiling joists.

It saves an incredible amount of time if you visualize your work before you do it—and it cuts way back on potential mistakes. Although this book presents a number of detailed drawings (see Figure 21), make yourself a sketch, complete with measurements. If you build three-dimensional models, that helps even more.

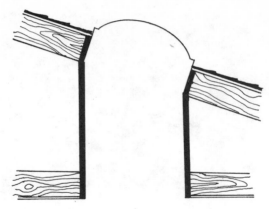

Vertical or Straight Shaftway, in which the roof opening is directly above the ceiling opening — and the same size.

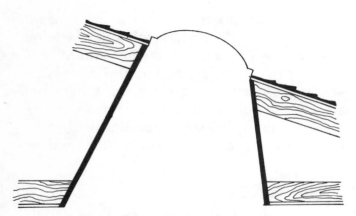

Conical or Splayed Shaftway, in which the ceiling opening is enlarged, offers greater light exposure.

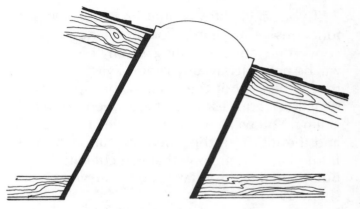

Angled or Tilted Shaftway, in which the shaft walls are angled to bypass pipes, ductwork, or roofline limitations.

The easiest way to build these walls is to assemble them on the floor and install them as separate units. For the angled walls, measure the length of the wall at the base and cut a two-by-three to this length. (Note that the actual measurements of the so-called two-by-three's are 1½" × 2⅝".) Measure the high and low points of the shaft wall and cut two-by-three's to these measurements. Lay out the wall studs, including any extra studs needed for nail blocks. Use the base plate as a guide for positioning the two-by-three's.

(Working indoors frequently means having a cramped work area. Inquisitive children and pets are notorious for causing problems, so be sure they are kept at a distance.)

An easy rule of thumb for sizing studs: add the length of the tallest stud and the shortest stud; divide by 2 for the length of the middle stud. This method works, no matter what the angle of the roof! By the same token, add the length of the longest and middle studs and divide by 2 to get the length of the stud between the longest and the middle stud. Divide by 4 to get the length of the stud between the shortest and the middle.

For example, if your longest stud is 12 inches, and your shortest is 8 inches, add the

Installing an APC Corporation ventilating skylight. Note the horizontal header (at left) and vertical studs, to which drywall will be nailed.

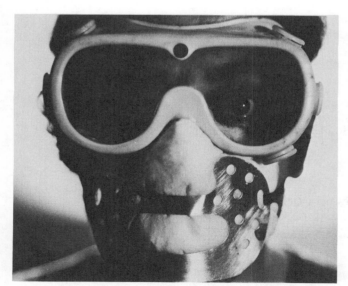

Goggles and mask protect against wood chips and airborne particles of insulation and drywall.

lengths together. 8 + 12 = 20. Divide by 2. 20 ÷ 2 = 10. Your middle stud should be 10 inches long. Easy, right? For instance, if the tallest stud is 20 inches, and the shortest one is 6 inches, you have (20 + 6) ÷ 2 = 13 inches.

All of the studs on the top of the skylight (the side closest to, and parallel to the crest of the roof) will be the same size, as will the bottom studs. Cut one trial stud for the top and one for the bottom, and use those as templates for the others.

Your top and bottom plates, as well as the shaftwall studs, should be made of 2" × 3" material. Use 2" × 6" lumber in the corners, so that later, you have an area wide enough to nail drywall without having to patch together a bunch of scrap. Save the 2" × 6" sections of joists that you have cut out for use as corner pieces in your shaftway frame. You can see by the drawings that there could be a problem where the top plate meets the header. The gap between the stud wall and the roof rafter could be shimmed out so the top plate is snug with all the roof joists. But if you have a pitched roof,

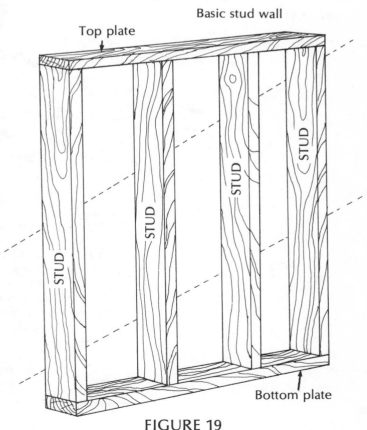

Basic stud wall

Top plate

STUD

STUD

STUD

STUD

Bottom plate

FIGURE 19

it's better to make angular cuts. The job is much easier and more professional if you use two simple tools: an adjustable square and a miter box. The adjustable square—as its name implies—adjusts to let you measure and mark angles other than 90 degrees. A good square should be marked in degrees and should be easy to adjust.

To get the angle of the cut, drop the plumb line from anywhere on the roof joists, measure the angle with your square, and set the angle on your miter box. Put your board into the miter box, and cut off the end. *Voilà!* Your board will now fit snugly in place against the roof joists without requiring unsightly wedges.

No matter what the *length* of your side-wall studs, the *angle* at the top of each board remains the same. Therefore, once you get the correct angle locked into your miter box, *don't change it!*

After you miter your corners, you will be left with little triangular scraps that are just perfect for nailing into the *outside* corners between joists and headers. This job involves almost no time or effort, but it will significantly improve the structural rigidity of your skylight

shaft. (Not all scrap wood is scrap. In my garage, I have an entire collection of odd-sized pieces of wood. Most get recycled for new projects. Even little, tiny scraps, when put in an ordinary, brown-paper grocery bag, make great kindling for a winter fire. Never throw out *anything* until you are certain that it can't be used somewhere else.)

Cut the pieces in your basement so you don't have to lug the tools into the attic. But building shaft walls in the basement is like trying to build a sailboat in your living room; you may do a great job, only to discover that the finished product is too big to fit through the doorway.

When you mark your boards, write down

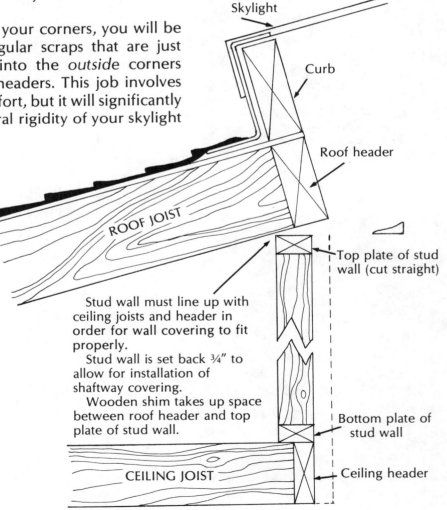

Skylight

Curb

Roof header

ROOF JOIST

Top plate of stud wall (cut straight)

Stud wall must line up with ceiling joists and header in order for wall covering to fit properly.

Stud wall is set back ¾" to allow for installation of shaftway covering.

Wooden shim takes up space between roof header and top plate of stud wall.

Bottom plate of stud wall

Ceiling header

CEILING JOIST

FIGURE 20

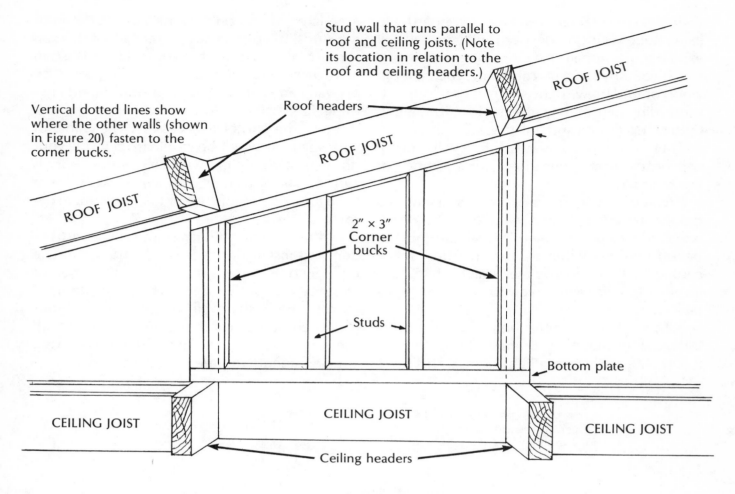

Stud wall that runs parallel to roof and ceiling joists. (Note its location in relation to the roof and ceiling headers.)

ROOF JOIST

Roof headers

ROOF JOIST

Vertical dotted lines show where the other walls (shown in Figure 20) fasten to the corner bucks.

ROOF JOIST

ROOF JOIST

2" × 3" Corner bucks

Studs

Bottom plate

CEILING JOIST

CEILING JOIST

CEILING JOIST

Ceiling headers

FIGURE 21

what your markings *mean*. That way you won't bring your boards up to the attic, only to get utterly confused.

Then put them together in the attic. Your stud wall may not fit if you don't trial-fit it first. Set the bottom plate down, set in the side-wall studs and corners, and set the top plate on top. If you took your time and measured everything correctly, it should fit without any problems. If so, remove everything, nail the assembly together, and then nail that to the joists and headers. If it doesn't fit, make the necessary changes and try another trial fit.

The only part of this construction that may present some problem is the corner (See Figure 22). When you erect the wall, be careful that there is a surface for fastening the wall covering. Check the drawing for ways to build these "corner bucks."

Just as you spliced in headers on the roof to support the curb, you will have to splice them in on the ceiling to support the shaftwalls. You will also have to cut out the center portion of the ceiling joist(s) directly below where you removed the roof rafters. *Frame in the ceiling hole with lumber of the same dimensions you used on your ceiling joists.* Do this either by building a curb whose outside dimensions equal the inside dimensions of the hole, or by nailing each side of the inside curb individually. Pre-assemble the curb if you can shanghai a couple of helpers to hold up the curb while you nail it in. If you work alone, the weight of a completed curb would be too much for you to hold, so nail in each piece one at a time.

It would be very discouraging to do a dynamite job on the outside, and then have the inside resemble something constructed by Moe, Larry, and Curly. A quality job is *thorough*. When constructing the ceiling curb, use your level frequently to ensure your boards are level. Keep your boards even, and your job will exude professionalism.

If you drive in nails carelessly, you can split wood or end up with the sharp ends of the nails protruding in unsightly places. Hit nails straight, then take a punch and sink the nail heads about 1/32" below the wood's surface. That will prevent nail heads from interfering with clearance of the boards.

You *don't* want your boards assembled crookedly; even a slight variation in angle on one stud can cause the entire wall assembly to be off-line. So when nailing in studs, make certain that the boards are straight. Use your level and square extensively to ensure an accurate fit.

To show you where the framing studs are for hanging the drywall, mark the bottom of the ceiling curb with a light pencil. This saves

time later when you'll want to locate the middle studs. In corners, it's better to be safe than sorry. Make sure each corner has at least an inch of nailing surface on each side of it, so drywall can be attached. You don't need anything fancy here—just nail an extra two-by-three to the corner if necessary. The frame of your shaftway won't be visible from inside your house, but you might want to paint the boards with a coat of primer or sealer to keep them from absorbing moisture or falling victim to dry rot.

If you want angular shaftwalls, construction and installation is basically the same. The only big difference is that almost all the boards will need extensive mitering. If you desire a more esoteric shaftwall design, measure your proposed angles carefully, and proceed with the steps outlined in this chapter, allowing yourself adequate time to execute the plan.

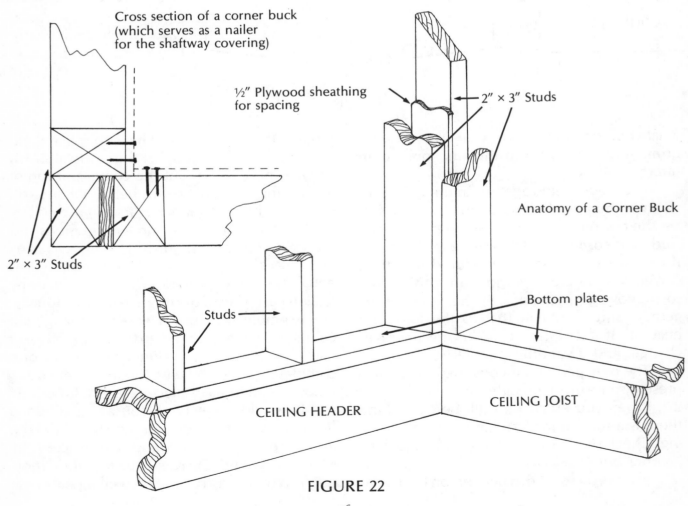

Cross section of a corner buck
(which serves as a nailer
for the shaftway covering)

1/2" Plywood sheathing
for spacing

2" × 3" Studs

Anatomy of a Corner Buck

2" × 3" Studs

Studs

Bottom plates

CEILING HEADER

CEILING JOIST

FIGURE 22

9 Electric Work:
Installing Lighting in Your Shaftway

Using a shaftway to conceal the light source, you can create very appealing lighting designs. If you have installed your skylight in a hallway, for example, *flush mounted* lights can create the same atmosphere at night as you enjoy during the day.

If you decide to install lighting, consider *where* you want it and *what type* you prefer. Incandescent light—the type produced by an ordinary light bulb—is the most common. Incandescent bulbs are also the cheapest and simplest: you install a socket and screw in your choice of many styles and colors of light bulbs. You could even put your Christmas tree under the skylight, and light up the shaftway with green and red!

If you want your plants to grow a little quicker, replace your incandescent bulbs with Gro-Lites, which look just like regular bulbs, but give off ultraviolet light. Leave them on for a couple hours each night, and you'll be amazed how your plants flourish—particularly during winter, when natural sunlight is in short supply. If the bulbs flicker out, check them in another socket before discarding. If they work in one socket but not the other, the problem is with the socket.

If you want recessed incandescent light in your shaftway walls, cut a circular hole in your drywall, using an old coffee can as a template. Drill a hole through the bottom of the coffee can large enough to fasten the socket to, and press-fit the assembly into the hole. (Make sure your power source is located so you can reach inside the shaft wall to plug in these lights.) For perfect support, attach some scrap wood perpendicularly to the adjacent shaftwall studs.

This is a simple, inexpensive solution that looks great. In the skylight I built in my bathroom, I wanted a light that wouldn't blind me when I turned it on after I just woke up. The way I solved this problem was really easy and incredibly cheap (about $2.50).

Reflector hoods come in a variety of shapes and sizes. The two I bought were about 4″ in diameter and about 7″ deep, with simple push-button light sockets. In the shaftway's wall covering, I cut a hole exactly matching the outside diameter of the reflector hoods, then pushed the hoods into the holes. Each hood has a lip at the edge that works as a stop and makes the job look finished. Since these lights come with standard plugs, I installed a single rectangular box with a duplex receptacle as my power source. Here I did not have to mount the box to the wall, since the plugs for the lights were inside the attic. The drawings in Figure 23 show exactly how the installation was done.

The higher you place a light in the shaftway, the dimmer and less obtrusive it becomes —and the more it will resemble natural light. By the same token, a low-wattage (45 to 75 watt), "soft white" bulb will give the same effect. So to make artificial light seem as natural as

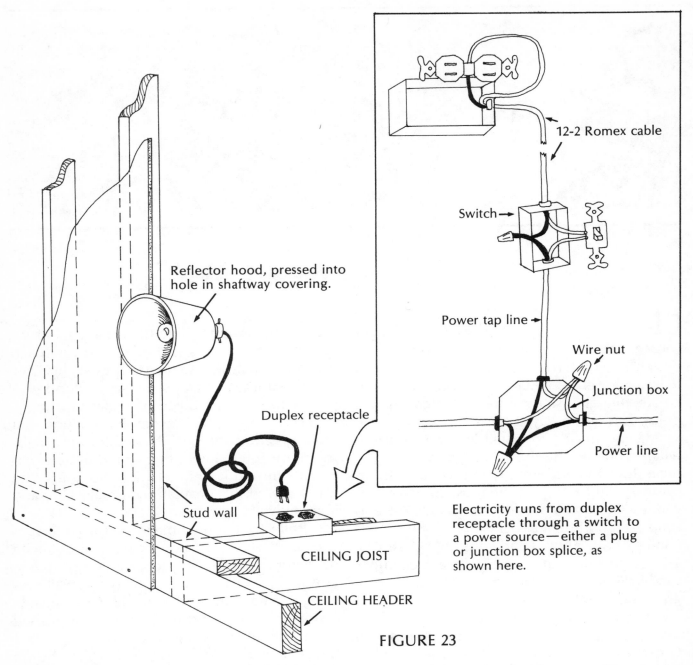

Reflector hood, pressed into hole in shaftway covering.

12-2 Romex cable

Switch

Power tap line

Wire nut

Junction box

Power line

Duplex receptacle

Stud wall

CEILING JOIST

CEILING HEADER

Electricity runs from duplex receptacle through a switch to a power source—either a plug or junction box splice, as shown here.

FIGURE 23

possible, place a soft-white, low-wattage bulb towards the top of the shaft. For bright light, use a high-wattage (100 to 150 watt) bulb near the bottom of the shaft.

A mirrored shaftway wall (see wall covering section) combined with a light bulb and a reflector cap on the opposite wall produces spectacular effects—especially with tinted light bulbs. A pale blue glow reflected off a row of mirrors adds an eerie but inviting, cathedral-like ambience to a room. Consider using swivel-type sockets such as those used for spotlights—again, your hardware dealer can help here. A

swivel socket can move 360 degrees, letting you aim the light exactly the way you want it.

Fluorescent bulbs cost more than incandescent ones, and don't come in as many different styles and types. But fluorescent light is totally different from an ordinary incandescent bulb's; it fills the room with a soft, moonlight glow, especially nice at night. Fluorescent lights can be hung vertically, as well as horizontally, so experiment with different placements before you mount your lights permanently.

Are any businesses moving or going under in your town? See if they are selling their light fixtures. A few years ago, I bought four 2' × 3' fluorescent fixtures, complete with bulbs and sockets, for under $15. With a little scrounging, you can find similarly cheap prices. The special fluorescent light sockets (known as ballasts) tend to rust around the bulb contacts, so if you plan to use these bulbs in a high-humidity area like a bathroom, check the contacts periodically.

Want *really* wild lighting in your skylight? Look into neon. Some stores specialize exclusively in neon lights. Although it's the most expensive type of light, with some careful shopping, you can find some real bargains. If you don't know where to look, ask the owner of a bar or restaurant with a neon light where he bought it.

AN ELECTRICAL CHECKLIST

If you need electrical outlets for lighting in your skylight, put them in *after* the framing has gone up, but *before* the wall covering goes on. To supply your skylight with electricity, you'll need:

Cable, known in the trade as Romex, is a plastic-sheathed cable with two conductors and a ground wire. The conductor wire comes in different thicknesses, or gauges. For this purpose, a 12-gauge conductor is right. When you buy cable, ask for "12-2 Romex"—which means Romex cable with two 12-gauge conductor wires.

Cable clamps are used where the Romex enters the box to provide a smooth surface (rather than the sharp edge of the box) for securing the cable.

Electrical boxes, of fabricated steel, come in several shapes (square, octagonal, or rectangular) and are supplied with stamped knockout plugs so the cable can be fed into the box easily. Some boxes have removable sides, allowing them to be joined (ganged) together. Others have specially designed brackets so they can be nailed or screwed to a stud or joist. Some have drill holes instead of brackets; sheet metal screws (1" #10 type) fasten the box to the stud or joist through these holes.

Plugs (in case you don't want to tap in at a junction box) are used to connect the appliance (the skylight outlets) to the power source.

Receptacles come in either a single or duplex style. They are constructed to receive a plug from an appliance or light fixture.

Switches connect and disconnect electrical current from its power source.

Wire nuts, funnel-shaped metal springs encased in heavy plastic, are a lot better than tape for wrapping electrical connections. They hold better, last longer, and won't come loose as tape can. Also, they come in three standard sizes. The large size is good for splicing three wires together.

Remember, a light must have a switch to control the circuit. You'll want to be able to turn the lights in your shaftway on and off, but stay away from dimmer switches. Although handy, they take more electricity to run bulbs at low-illumination. Instead, run a series of switches to cut off one or two lights at a time.

Before you begin wiring, figure out where you want your light switch. Now, where will you tap into the house's power? The simplest solution is to replace an existing *single* light switch with a double switch. Just make sure there's enough room behind the wall for you to run the new cable.

Another way to bring power to the skylight is to build what amounts to a permanent extension cord. The third way is to splice into one of the junction boxes located in the attic. For both the permanent extension cord and the junction-box splice, the basic plan is the same. The

Duplex receptacle box, before and after installation.

circuit goes from an outlet box with a duplex receptacle—fastened to a convenient location near the skylight—through the cable to a switch (to control the lights) and from there to the power supply. Look at the drawing carefully; see the sequence in which the circuit is built. The most difficult part is finding a location for the switch. It's no problem running the cable through the attic and the shaft walls. But when it comes to finding a spot on the existing wall to mount the switch box, things get a little tricky.

The easy way is to locate your switch box in a stud wall, since then you have a ready-made channel for the cable. First, cut a hole in the wall for the switch box. Next, drill a hole in the top plate of the wall and feed your wire through this hole. Fish another piece of wire through the switch box hole. Install the switch box, feeding the cable through and securing it to the wall with a cable clamp. (Be sure to use the right type switch box for your walls. There is a box specially made for drywall and also one for plaster lathe.)

INSTALLING ELECTRICAL JUNCTION BOXES AND LIGHT SWITCHES

This is perhaps the easiest part of working on a skylight. The only real difficulty lies in the danger of electricity. The one and only *right*

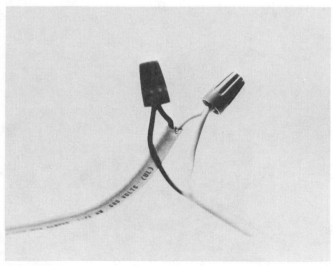

Wire nuts in use.

way to avoid French-frying yourself is to *shut off all power where you will be working.* Double-check the circuit breaker box to make certain.

Although you will be working indoors with the power off, *don't* install your wiring if there's the possibility of lightning. A few years ago, a Florida woman was killed when one of her electrical appliances exploded during a thunderstorm. Though the odds of such a disaster occurring are minimal, it would be no consolation if you got zapped.

After you install the switch, following the wiring diagram in Figure 23, attach your cable to the power supply. Here is where the difference between the two power-supply methods arises. With the permanent extension cord, you simply plug the cable into an existing outlet. I prefer the junction-box splice method, however, because it makes the whole job look more professional. It may be a little difficult, but if you follow the steps below, you should have no problem splicing into a junction box.

1. Locate the nearest junction box in your attic—ideally, one in a convenient location.

2. Here you will need a flashlight. *Shut off all the circuits or fuses in the house.* When all the power is off, remove the covering of the spliced wires. Add another cable clamp by punching out one of the knock-outs. Slide in your cable. Strip off the protective covering, baring just the ends of the wires.

3. Separate the groups of wires.

4. Join each wire to its appropriate group, matching the colors (black to black, white to white)—with either a larger wire nut or a good wrapping of plastic electrical tape.

5. Push the bunches of wires back into the junction box and replace the cover plate.

6. Turn the power back on.

If you decide to use the plug method, instead of running the cable to a junction box after it passes the switch, just run it to the nearest receptacle. Since you have to mount the cable on the outside of the walls to reach the plug, you may as well run all the switch wiring on the surface.

If you can't find a stud wall to run your cable through, and the only wall available is made of brick and plaster, then (1) cut a small channel in the plaster to let the cable run down, and (2) cut a hole in the plaster deep enough for a specially made box (that is not nearly so deep as a standard outlet). Repair the wall with patching plaster, and remember to sand and repaint it later.

Although installing lighting in your skylight may seem like a lot of work, the finished product is well worth the relatively little time spent.

SHAFTWALL INSULATION

After you've finished the electric work, insulate your skylight shaft. (If the rest of your attic is not already insulated, do it now. You will really be amazed at the difference. And remember to insulate every nook and cranny of the room while you're at it.) Before you insulate your skylight, though, find out which type of insulation will be most effective for your job. Remember that the effectiveness is determined not just by the type of insulation you use, but also by where and how you use it.

Sprayed foam insulation is becoming more popular. A professional insulator sprays foam between the studs, and the foam hardens to form a barrier between the attic air and the walls. While foam insulation works well, its complexity and expense don't make it worthwhile for such a small area. Behind your shaftway walls, use fiberglass *roll insulation*, which comes in different widths, thicknesses, and R-values (ratings assigned by the manufacturer to indicate the products' relative insulating capacity). The higher the R-value, the more effective the insulation. But *don't* automatically buy the insulation with the highest R-value; specific R-values are manufactured for specific climates. To find roll insulation that meets your

climate's needs, see what your local supplier recommends.

In roll insulation, the fiberglass is held together by either foil or kraft paper. Either kind will work quite well. The type with the foil back costs more than kraft paper backing, but helps reflect the heat back into the house.

Roll insulation also comes in two standard thicknesses—3½" and 6". But just because one piece of insulation is thicker, don't assume that it will insulate better. Remember, it's the R-value, not the thickness, that determines insulating power. Depending on the space between your studs, you can buy roll insulation in two widths, 15½" and 24". Once you know the width you need, cut the stuff to the necessary length (the height of the shaftwall) with a mat knife guided by a straightedge. Insert the strip of insulation between the studs. All insulation comes with flaps along both edges, just staple the flaps to the studs, and the job is done.

Tape the seams of your roll insulation in the shaftway where it meets the shaftway studs. I would recommend applying weather-stripping tape. (3-M and a number of other manufacturers make a high-quality, inexpensive product.) This will give you a much tighter seal, which minimizes air transfer and saves energy. When using tape insulation, pay particular attention to the corners and small cracks—the most likely sources of air leaks. If you aren't sure whether a section of your wall is fully sealed, apply a little extra tape as insurance. Wasting 50 cents' worth of tape is still cheaper than wasting $5 worth of heat every month.

Insulation is an important—and too often overlooked—part of skylight installation. It does more than keep your house warmer in the wintertime; insulation minimizes temperature fluctuations the year around. Insulation keeps air from one section of your house from leaking into another. It's just like having a cap on a bottle: the tighter the seal, the less leakage you have, and the better it works. Ideally, a skylight should save you money, not waste it, and a few simple hints will make your skylight energy-efficient.

10 Covering the Shaftway with Drywall

Now that you have the skylight framed, supplied with power, and insulated, how are you going to cover the studs? Your existing ceiling is probably plaster or drywall. In either case, putting drywall on the new framing can be an economical and attractive way to finish your walls.

In covering your shaftway, hanging drywall is the first step. Mirrors, paneling, or paint must all wait until later. The beauty of this is that you don't have to make a final wallcovering commitment until after the drywall is up. Six months later, should you decide to put paneling over the drywall, you are free to do so. (Other alternatives for finishing the framed shaftway are suggested in the next section.)

Like most of the other supplies used in this project, drywall comes in a number of forms. Waterproof drywall is popular today, but despite its high quality, the high cost makes it the wrong choice unless your skylight is in the bathroom. If you are worried about possible water damage, give ordinary drywall a good coat of sealer, which serves the same purpose for a lot less money.

NECESSARY TOOLS

Before the work begins, let's go over the tools that will make the drywall job easier:

Drywall saw is a must if you have to cut openings in the drywall for electric boxes. It makes the job quick and the results satisfactory.

Drywall trowel—I use three trowels: (1) a five-inch trowel for scooping drywall paste into the pan and for doing first-coat work; (2) an all-purpose model 12 inches long with a very flexible blade for taping seams and applying second and third coats of the paste over the nails; and (3) a trowel bent at a 90° angle that flexes easily, making inside corner work go like a breeze.

Mud pan carries small amounts of drywall paste so you don't have to dip into the large can any more than necessary.

Sandpaper—You'll need 80-grit paper to smooth the hardened paste over the drywall.

Straightedge—There's a square available with a 4-foot leg, but unless you're going to do a lot of drywall, spend your money elsewhere. Instead, use a nice straight piece of 1" × 4" pine. For long lines, use a chalk line.

Once you've gotten your tools together, you can get to work.

CUTTING, HANGING, AND FINISHING

As with every other phase of construction, the first step in drywall hanging is accurate measurement. Visualize where each piece of drywall will go. Are you sure you have enough nailing space in the corners to attach the drywall? Leave yourself a little extra material at the bottom of the shaftway. Unlike the sides and top, the bottom is best trimmed *after* the drywall is hung, to ensure an even finish where the shaftway meets the ceiling.

After you have measured the drywall, start cutting it. Notice that drywall is composed of three layers. The top and bottom are a cardboardlike product that gives substance to the thick center of gypsum. Use your square or straightedge as a guide for cutting through the top layer. First, use a mat knife to score the top layer and break the center gypsum layer. Next, score the back side, then snap the drywall back to get a nice, even break.

Test-fit each piece before you hang it, using your level to ensure that the pieces are straight. Don't forget to cut out holes for light sockets and switches. Measure the position of the socket or switch on the wall, then draw a pattern on the drywall and cut. It's much easier to cut the drywall before it's hung, than after it's up in the shaftway.

Ready to nail? Be sure you have all the nailers in place. (Check the corners carefully.) The proper fasteners to use are special drywall nails, blue in color (a coating to inhibit rust), with a large head, and ridged to keep them from pulling out. When you hang the drywall, drive the nails so the hammer "dimples" the drywall's surface. (Try not to break the surface paper of the drywall.) Dimpling enables you to cover the head of the nail with drywall paste so that the finished surface will be completely even.

The tighter you butt the drywall sections together, the easier they'll be to work with. Drywall paste contracts a bit as it dries, and gaps wider than ¼" between pieces will cause the drywall tape to pucker, leaving a nasty-looking ripple in the wall.

The only thing left is to cover the seams (not as difficult as it may sound). Drywall paste comes ready-mixed or in bags. I think the ready-mix variety is best—there is absolutely no hassle and much less mess and clean-up. Don't forget to leave a dropcloth under your work area: no sense in ruining your carpet or hardwood floor. If you do spill drywall paste on your floor or walls, the best way to remove it is with cold, clean water, as soon as it happens. Since the paste is water-soluble, it comes off quickly

and easily if wiped up right away. But the longer it stays on, the harder it is to remove.

Drywall tape is used with the paste to cover drywall seams. Using the 5" trowel, first apply the coating of paste to the seams. After the paste is down, center one end of the tape over the joint and press the rest of the tape firmly into the paste.

As you pull the trowel along, the paste should ooze out slightly from under the tape. Don't press *too* hard, or *all* the paste will squeeze out and you won't get a good bond between tape and drywall.

One of the easiest ways to guarantee a good drywall and paste job is to clean your drywall trowels constantly. Dirt and drywall particles quickly mar the drywall surface, and trying to remove them is exasperating (and probably futile). So if the paste becomes dirty, discard it. The advantage of using a pan is that only a small amount needs to be thrown away.

To avoid wrinkles and puckers like that of the too-wide seam, apply the tape slowly and evenly. If you've followed the directions so far, your skylight should look great. Don't blow all that work now on an easily preventable problem. And don't put on so much paste that you cover the tape on the first coat. By the time all three coats are on, the tape will have neatly disappeared.

Give drywall paste 24 hours to dry between coats. Don't rush the pasting, since it will take a couple of days no matter how fast you go. Take the time to bury the seams completely, and

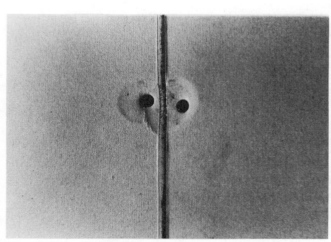

A properly dimpled drywall seam.

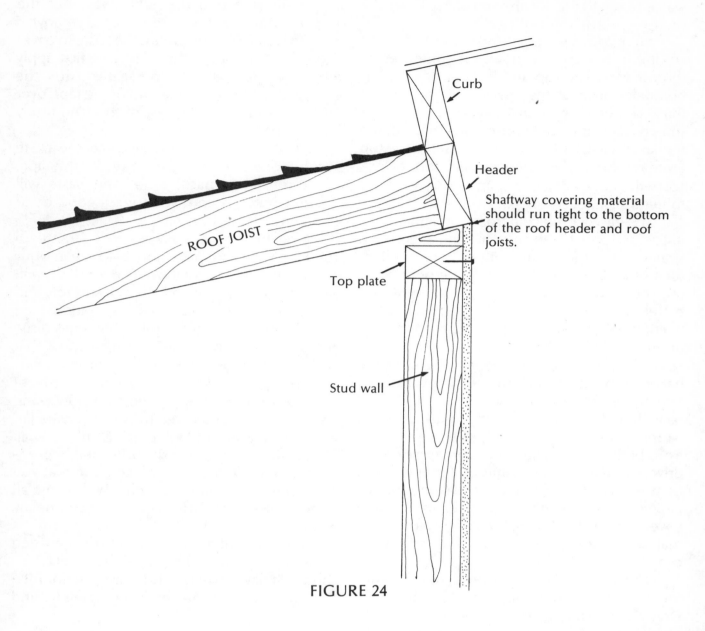

Curb

Header

Shaftway covering material should run tight to the bottom of the roof header and roof joists.

ROOF JOIST

Top plate

Stud wall

FIGURE 24

your work will look much better. After the first coat is dry, apply a second or filler coat. Using the same material with a wider trowel, spread the paste a couple of inches on both sides of the taped seam, feathering out toward the edge. *Again, don't use too much paste.* It is easier to fill in a dip than it is to sand down lumps of dry paste.

When the second coat is dry, sand it *lightly*. Too much pressure results in uneven seams or,

worse yet, sanding right through the drywall tape. Then put on the third or trim coat to fill in the recesses and smooth the joints to a finished quality. If there are any minor imperfections left in the third coat, a final sanding should take care of them.

The only thing you have to watch out for is the seam that is not tapered. If you have cut seams, or if you have cut the short edge of a full sheet, there will be no tapered end. Here the

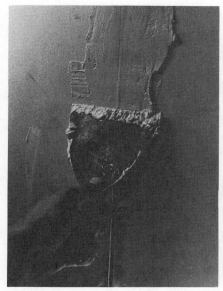

Applying the first coat of drywall paste over the seam.

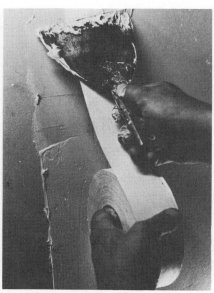

Applying the drywall tape.

After a second coat of paste, the tape begins to disappear.

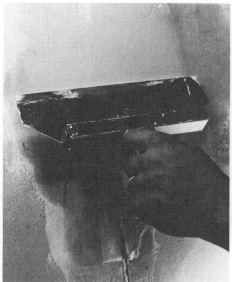

Apply the finishing coat with a wide-blade trowel.

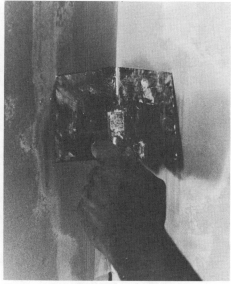

For applying tape and paste to corners, use a special trowel like this.

trick is to make the feathered edge wider so that the hump created by the lack of a tapered edge will disappear. To do this, work through the same steps as for the tapered edges.

To tape an *inside corner,* measure the correct amount of drywall tape and fold the tape in half. Apply a first coat of paste on both sides of the corner. Position the tape in the corner and use the corner trowel to press down the tape securely. Use the wide trowels to feather the

seam, as with the tapered edge. The *outside corner* is finished with a product called metal-cornerbead, so that the corner won't be damaged if bumped. This bead is nailed in place with drywall nails.

Feather both sides of the corner with increasingly wider coats of drywall paste; sand smooth between coats. Finish over nail dimples with the same three-coat process, sanding between coats.

11 Completing the Shaftway

Thermal glass consists of two sheets of glass joined together at the edges with a rubber sealant. The vacuum in the space between the two pieces insulates the window against heat loss. (The fewer air molecules in between, the more efficient the insulation will be.) However, thermal-pane glass is very expensive, especially in larger sizes. You can avoid the expense of thermal glass by making an internal storm window that works on the same principle. The air trapped between the two frames of either Plexiglas or plate glass will act as an insulator between the outer temperature and the inner temperature.

INTERNAL STORM WINDOWS

You can fit an internal storm window near the top of your skylight shaft, at the bottom, or anywhere in between. If it's located at the bottom of the shaft, it can be illuminated by lights inside the shaftway, which may not appeal to you, because at the bottom of the shaftway the storm window obscures the shaftway itself. But if you're using an internal storm window that's tinted or translucent, you need only one coat of paint on the shaftway drywall —thus eliminating the expense of paneling or wallpaper.

There are two easy ways to build an internal storm window. In both cases, first nail a 1″ × 2″ pine strip on the edge around the inside of the curb so the top of the strip touches the skylight. Figure 15 shows exactly where this pine strip should be nailed. If you know for sure you will use a storm window, nail on the pine strip when you install the curb.

For a skylight used primarily for illumination, as in a workshop or studio, you can just staple some plastic sheeting to the strip. If you want, put a cover strip over the staples, as in Figure 25. Remember that although the plastic sheet does let the light in, it is not completely transparent.

Another method will solve the insulation problem and still let you look up at the world. After nailing the pine strip in place, cut a piece of Plexiglas to the same measurements as the inside of the curb. Then drill holes about every twelve to fourteen inches around the perimeter of the Plexiglas for the wood screws that will fasten the Plexiglas to the bottom of the pine strip. Then, before you screw the storm window in place, install a piece of weatherstripping around the bottom of the batten. Use strips of felt nailed in place with small brads, or strip rubber, which comes in a roll and has an adhesive back. Peel off the protective tape and press the strip into place. You can drill pilot holes for the screws right through both types of weatherstripping. (Also see Figures 15 and 17.)

For skylights larger than nine square feet, you should use $^{3}/_{16}$″ Plexiglas. For smaller skylights, $^{1}/_{8}$″ will work fine. Remember, it isn't the thickness of the material that insulates the sky-

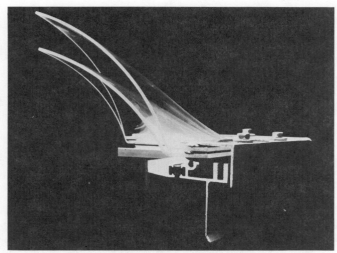

Two layers of plastic in Naturalite's "thermalized" bubble retard heat loss.

light, but the layer of trapped air.

You can install an internal storm window permanently, but it makes sense to make it removable. You need only 2" quarter-round material and a sheet of glass or Plexiglas cut 1" smaller than the inside dimensions of your curb. Nail the quarter-round to the curb, slide the storm window inside and over the quarter-rounds, and you're finished.

This arrangement is by far the most cost-efficient and beautiful way to solve the storm window dilemma—two advantages that don't usually go together. The nicest part is that you can remove the storm window for cleaning or replacement. If you construct a removable internal storm window and don't want as much sun in your home during the summer, you can replace the transparent Plexiglas with either white or translucent off-white Plexiglas to block out the sun without losing the look of natural light. You can also use stained glass or tinted Plexiglas for your internal storm window, giving the shaftway some rather wild and beautiful effects. If you ever get tired of one color storm window, put in another. You can even change them seasonally. For instance, use clear Plexiglas in winter to admit the most light and heat, and a translucent sheet in the summer. While the removable storm window sacrifices some thermal efficiency, it keeps your options as broad as possible—which is one reason for having a skylight in the first place.

Putting the internal storm window towards the top of the skylight gives you an unobstructed view of the shaftway, which adds a sense of expansion to the room—in other words, your home looks bigger. You can still use lights below the internal window, although the effect isn't as dramatic.

Which method is best? Only you can judge that. Before you finish the drywall, try lightly nailing your quarter-rounds at a few different places along the shaftway, and go with what looks best to *you*. Conceivably, you could even run the internal storm window at an angle to your ceiling, but parallel to the pitch of your roof.

STAINED GLASS UNDER YOUR SKYLIGHT

Although genuine stained glass can be hideously expensive, bargains abound for the astute shopper who knows where to look. You should investigate as many local second-hand shops, garage sales, and glass suppliers as possible before committing yourself to the going tariff. Above all, make sure you know the exact size you need before you start shopping.

Also check with your local hobby store for kits to assemble your own stained glass. Finding

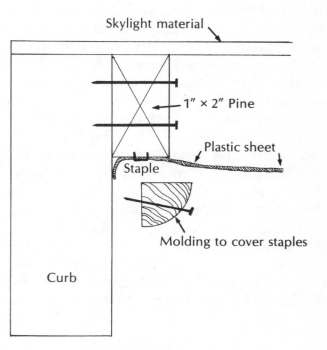

FIGURE 25

out how to do it ahead of time will give you a better idea of the cost and complexity involved. Get several stores' recommendations as to the best kits. A good one should include logical instructions, quality materials, and a competitive price—though you shouldn't be too concerned with price as long as the materials and quality are up to snuff.

Use extreme caution when working with glass; it takes very little effort to slice yourself badly. Don't use any tool other than a specially made glass cutter, which isn't very expensive but is easy to use. Simply scribe a line where you want to cut, lay a towel over the glass, and break it by applying even pressure to both halves.

Nothing diminishes the fun of working with stained glass more than a sliced artery. To protect your hands, always wear gloves while cutting. It's also a good idea to wear goggles, in case a piece shatters.

MAKING THE PLEXIGLAS TINT GEL

This is an amazingly simple way to bring "stained" or tinted light into your home. All you need is Plexiglas and spray paint manufactured for use on *plastic* model cars and planes, not for wooden ones; you can find it at any toy or hobby store. If you want a transparent gel, buy transparent final coat paint. The exact labeling varies from brand to brand, but the can should say something like "clear-tint coat." These transparent paints give only a color without blocking any light.

Peel the protective covering off one side of the Plexiglas, and—following the directions on the label—apply the spray paint in a smooth, thin coat. If you apply one thick layer, it dries unevenly and doesn't look good; it's always better to apply a number of thin coats.

This poor man's version of stained glass is quite attractive. If you are handy with a spray can, you can get really tricky by combining colors or "fogging" the edges so that the center of the Plexiglas is almost clear, while the

Stained glass roundel doubles as an interior storm window.

outsides get progressively darker. After the paint has dried, peel the covering off the other side of the Plexiglas and install the sheet as described in the "Internal Storm Windows" section.

This gel tint is a natural for use with mirrors and lights. You can even make a couple of different colors of tints to see what looks best. For the ultimate in cathedral-style psychedelia, cut one large sheet of Plexiglas into a number of smaller pieces. Spray each piece a different color, then glue them back together with capillary cement to hide the seams. Your skylight will look like it came from the Middle Ages— or from another world.

12 Finishing the Drywall

Once the storm window is up, you are faced with the pleasant dilemma of having to choose what to cover the drywall with—a dilemma only because the choices are so mind-boggling. You can use paint, paneling, wallpaper, mirrors, ceramic tile, wood parquet . . . the list goes on and on. Realistically, though, your most important consideration is finding a wall covering that fits *your* decor aesthetically. You want a wall covering that enhances your *existing* decor, without forcing you to remodel the room. (In other words, avoid wretched excess—unless the room is *already* finished in wretched excess.) If you have a slate floor, for example, I wouldn't recommend using wood on your shaftway walls—for the simple reason they won't look natural unless there's wood on the floor below.

No matter what ideas anyone else gives you, don't assume what's right for one skylight is necessarily right for yours. Once the drywall is hung, what looks best in your home is a matter of what looks good to *you*. You have the luxury of being able to take your time to shop around and find the wallcovering solution that's most compatible with your wallet, skill, and sense of design.

PAINT

This is the cheapest and easiest way to make your shaftway as handsome as the light shining through it. If you can put in a skylight, you probably don't need a long discourse on painting techniques, so the tips here will be brief.

Buy the best quality paint you can find. Since your shaftway is going to be bombarded with light, stay away from cheap paint that will fade quickly. *Consumer Reports* and other publications periodically rate interior and exterior paints, and it might be worthwhile to hunt through their back issues to check. I would advise using latex paint; it's much cheaper than oilbased paint, a lot easier to work with, and a snap to clean up. Best of all, good latex paint will afford years of wear and quality.

If you are painting the shaftway drywall, you will also have to repaint the ceiling where it joins the shaftway. If your paint is a custom color, make certain you have an adequate supply on hand—or can get more. If your paint is no longer available, you may be better off painting the entire walls and ceiling a new color to avoid mismatches.

For under two dollars, you can purchase foam rubber corner-trimmers, which facilitate the otherwise unpleasant task of painting tight corners. If you don't finish painting all at once, you can postpone cleaning your brushes and trimmers by putting each in a plastic sandwich bag. Seal the bag, and then store it in the freezer. The paint won't dry, and after about five minutes to thaw out, the brush or trimmer can be used again.

OTHER KINDS OF WALL COVERINGS

The walls of your skylight shaft are not very long or very wide. Packing crate lumber is one of the cheaper convenient alternatives for finishing your skylight shaft, because it is generally available in appropriate lengths.

Is packing crate lumber a bit too rustic for you? Consider using random-width or uniform-size pine boards (1″ × 6″, for example). Pine boards can be laid diagonally for an attractive design. You can buy either #2 white pine, which has some knots, or clear white pine, which should have no knots. If you'd prefer not to lay down all those planks in a skylight shaft, wood paneling looks great and comes in many different grades, colors, and textures. The cheapest has a photographic overlay on a Masonite panel and tends to look like what it is—sloppy and cheap. Veneer paneling, with actual wood covering the panel, has the look and feel of real wood, and, if the color is right, makes a very suitable covering for shaftway walls.

Lumberyards usually have plenty of samples to show. I used to do a lot of interior remodeling for clients, and I quickly found that things look different at home than they do in the store. Rather than buying your paneling ahead of time, only to discover that it doesn't look good at home, take home some samples from the lumberyard to match and try out.

Paneling must be nailed to the studs *behind* the drywall. Don't nail at random; nail only where the studs are, and it will have something firm to hold on to and will stay in place. Remember how we spaced the nail holes at different intervals to avoid driving one nail on top of another? Do the same thing when you install the paneling.

The wall covering should run to the underside of the roof header, as shown in Figure 24. Unless you're using drywall and metal corner bead, the corner where the ceiling meets the shaftwall requires special treatment. Outside corner molding is generally used on paneled walls.

If you used planks of some sort, you can trim out the skylight with the same material (see

Shaftway planks should run vertically to emphasize the height.

Figure 26). The four inside corners can be dealt with in a couple of ways. First, cut the wall covering tight, so you get a good seam at the corners. The line created by the joining of the two should be straight. Alternatively, you can buy pre-milled molding made specifically for paneling. If you are using planks, you can finish the corners with narrow strips of the same material used for covering (See Figure 27.)

Remember, *anything* used as a wall covering can be used to cover the shaftway—and some things may work for the shaftway that couldn't work over an entire wall. A nice alternative to paneling is cork, which comes in sheets and individual tiles. Check with your hardware store for colors and prices. For an unusual shaft, you might want to use carpeting.

Wallpaper, though almost as expensive as paneling, looks nice in the shaftway—especially if your walls and ceiling are already papered. Avoid trying to mix and match patterns: use the same style wallpaper that's on your walls. Buy an extra roll or two, though, because wallpaper patterns change yearly, and it is important to be able to replace shaftway paper if it fades in a few years. Whatever you use for a wallcovering is going to be exposed to lots of sunlight, and as a result may fade more quickly than would normal interior wallpaper.

Without question, one of the most dynamic shaftway coverings is ceramic tile. Though the finished result is well worth it and particularly beautiful when the sun radiates off it, ceramic tile is more expensive and difficult to work with than any other wall covering. If you've got the money and the time, you should see what patterns are available, and how much work your shaftway would require. Home-improvement stores can provide you with the needed materials and instruction to do a great job. If you find a good tile shop or hardware store, ask about mirror tiles or whole mirror sections, which can dramatically increase the perceived size of your shaftway. Combined with lights and/or filters, mirrors add dazzle to a skylight at lower cost than ceramic tiles. You can mirror one or two walls and light the other walls for added reflection.

I would recommend that you pick up a general do-it-yourself reference book for home repairs, especially one with good ideas on more sophisticated types of wallcoverings like ceramic tile. Such books are broader in concept than this one, and may give you some appealing ideas—as well as serving as a handy refer-

Cork paneling.

ence for other home projects.

No matter what your wallcovering, your hardware store should have edge and corner trimmers in metal, wood, or plastic. They make the job look better, and meet the criteria for equipment used in this project—namely, inexpensive, easy to work with, and good-looking.

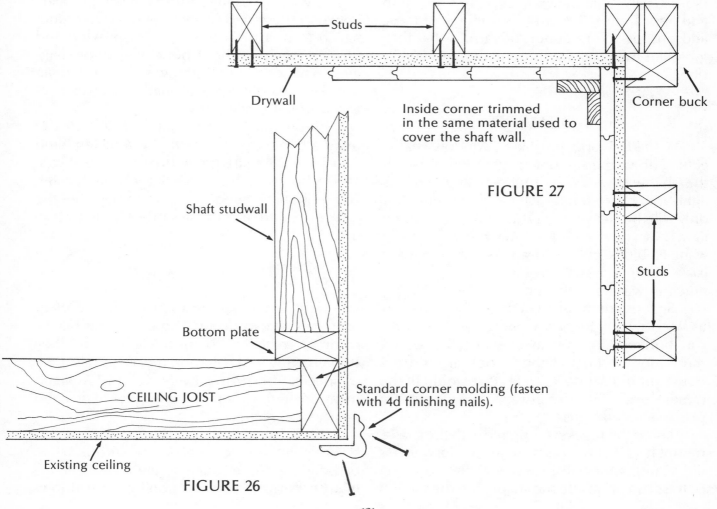

FIGURE 27

FIGURE 26

13 Accessories Under Your Skylight

Now that you've got the basics down pat, it's time to add a bit of high-tech sophistication, while still keeping the cost at bargain basement levels. Simple uses of baffles and shades can dramatically change your skylight's function and appearance. The great advantage of these add-ons, as you're about to learn, is that they *look* like they cost far more than they actually do.

BAFFLES AND SHADES

A *shade* works just like a window shade, cutting down the amount of light falling through the shaftway. A *baffle* redirects and reduces light, much like a filter on a camera lens. Not only will they let you block too-intense daytime light, but you can choose how *much* light you want to block out—a simple solution if your large skylight heats up your room a bit too much in warmer weather.

Shades are installed in much the same way as window shades, with one exception: they run horizontally instead of vertically, so you must modify them slightly. Look around the house for old window shades that would fit the dimensions of your shaftway, or else purchase pre-assembled units.

Using the brackets supplied with the shade, mount it so that the ends are in parallel walls (as illustrated). One half-inch below the mounting points, and ½" inside the shade, run the section of quarter-round molding parallel to the bottom of the shaftway and across the entire width of the shaft. A quarter inch below the first piece, run a piece of quarter-round the same size as you just used. Your shade will fit neatly between these two sections of quarter-round, which form a track in which it can wind and unwind freely, without bunching up or snagging. The only other thing you need is an accessible handle for your shade so you can roll and unroll it easily.

If you want to get a bit fancier, you can build a baffle from an ordinary venetian blind instead of the roll-type shade described above. The technique in both cases is the same, though you must allow adequate spacing between the quarter-round sections for the blinds to fold up.

PLANTS

Light is the key factor by which a plant produces its own food. And *all* species have a common reaction to insufficient light: they stop growing and will soon die. While a variety of species can do relatively well in low light, many (including most flowering plants) do need plenty of sunlight.

Yet in most rooms, the supply of light is severely limited. Perhaps nearby shrubs, trees, or buildings keep much sunlight from entering. Or perhaps you just don't have windows with a southern or eastern exposure: northern and western windows receive very little direct sun. If you can't grow all the species you'd like to, you could install fluorescent tubes, under which many kinds of sun-loving plants can thrive. Or you might consider placing them under your skylight.

Even though much of a room will not receive the sun's direct rays, the general improvement in the level of light makes it possible for you to add plants that need bright, indirect light. Given the brilliant light the unit should make available, you should be able to raise even the most light-hungry species. One gardener I know has created a mini-desert, filled with varieties of cacti, just below his skylight. Another has installed a small pool with water plants. With the sun falling through the skylight and hanging plants dangling from above, it looks like a tiny glade in a tropical rain forest.

Admittedly, adding a skylight to increase your selection of house plants may be far down your list of priorities. But if you've already decided on a skylight for other reasons, don't neglect the opportunity to add plants, which can produce stunning decorative effects.

After you've installed the skylight, mark out the path of sunlight across the room, from morning until sunset. Across the path, arrange the plants that need bright sunlight. Around it, place plants needing bright, but indirect, illumination. Because the light will be moving across the room, it won't linger in any spot long enough to damage plant leaves or blossoms. However, the area directly beneath the skylight may become much warmer than the rest of the room, and excessively high temperatures can damage plants.

Take a temperature reading right below the skylight when the sun is falling directly on that spot. Take another reading when the sun has moved on, and the spot beneath the skylight is left in indirect light. Place the thermometer at the same level as the tops of the majority of plants. If the temperature doesn't decrease very much after the sun has moved on, you'll have to take steps to protect the plants (misting them frequently will help). What seems a problem in the spring or summer can

Plants suspended from existing rafters. Drip-pans prevent spills when watering, and monofilament plastic fishline is strong, but barely visible.

become a benefit in winter, when extra warmth will be appreciated by any plants you're attempting to bring to blossom. But the angle of the sun will keep changing, and you'll need to rearrange the plants every month or so.

To avoid continual moves, you can suspend plants in baskets around the edges of the skylight and group light-loving plants right beneath the shaftway. Suspendable containers are available in an astonishing array of sizes, shapes, and colors. There are containers of glazed or unglazed clay, pots of brass or copper, plastic pots, and handwoven pots. Buy only ones that have a saucer attached beneath the drainage holes to catch run-off after each watering. Wire baskets, lined with strips of moss and then filled with soil, drip a good deal after each watering, making them impractical

To hang heavy plants, don't remove your rafters—just remove the roof and sheathing and cover the gap with a multi-paned dome.

off and may serve as a bridge for pests passing from plant to plant. Place the hooks along the edges of the skylight if the ceiling material is strong enough to support the weight. Otherwise, you'll have to suspend the containers from those rafter beams nearest the skylight.

Hanging large, heavy plants in a shaftway needn't be a problem. You can very easily construct a tripod chain to hang plants from; all you need are three screw hooks and chains.

Drill a small hole through the drywall into one of the shaftway studs. (If you only drill into the drywall and not the stud, your screw hooks won't hold.) Screw the screw hooks into the hole. The hooks' size is up to you, but a good rule of thumb is that the heavier the plant, the larger the hook you'll need. Repeat this on two of the other walls, so that you have screw hooks in three of the four walls. To suspend very large or very heavy containers, substitute molly bolts or toggles for the screw hooks.

Take sections of chain, hang them on each hook, and gather the bottoms together at the center of the shaftway. Insert the plant-holder through the bottom link of each section of chain, and you're finished. If the plant doesn't hang evenly, adjust the links until the plant is as level as you want it.

MOBILES

Mobiles look great in skylights, and are easy to make. You can buy them pre-assembled of course, but you can construct a mobile yourself from leftover glass or Plexiglas and monofilament fishing line. Simply epoxy a piece of monofilament between two pieces of glass or Plexiglas, and you have a hanging mobile section. For the "arms" of the mobile, use wire coat-hanger sections with the hooks removed. Tie the top of the monofilament lines to the ends of the coat-hangers, and you have an easy-to-construct mobile that's just as good-looking as a store-bought one. The fact that it's cheaper as well only makes the bargain better.

for use indoors—unless you want to suspend them over moisture-loving plants that will appreciate the frequent showers.

Containers can be suspended with any strong material: nylon or hemp ropes, thick woven ropes, leather thongs, chains, or strong wire. Use brackets, ceiling hooks, or side hooks to hang the container in place. But before setting any hooks, know the size of your containers and the width of the plants. Don't hang plants so closely that their foliage intermingles. This will cause shaded leaves to yellow or drop

14 Skylight Maintenance and Protection

Like the rest of your home, your skylight should be maintained on a regular basis. *Unlike* the rest of your house, this doesn't involve much work.

Twice a year, in the spring and fall, inspect the outside of your skylight for signs of wear. Pay close attention to caulking beads and roofing cement seams. If either of these areas looks dry or cracked, put another coat of the appropriate sealant on the bad spots. This is also a good time to clean the gutters and inspect the rest of your roof.

Twice a year you should inspect the *inside* of your roof as well. Go into the attic and make sure the insulation and the electrical systems are all tightly in place. Take care of any loose insulation or wiring. There should be no gaps in the shaftway walls where air can escape, causing lower energy efficiency.

If you live in an area prone to vandalism or crime, you have several ways to prevent your skylight from being damaged by fallen or thrown objects.

Wire glass, commonly found in schools and businesses, has wire screening running through the glass itself. Though durable, its primary function is to keep people from entering by breaking the glass. Since the wire is *inside* the glass, it will not stop the glass from shattering if hit by a rock or B.B. gun pellets.

Wire *outside* the glass is better protection against breakage. For that reason, constructing a screenguard for your skylight is a more effective way to reduce the possibility of damage —and it is more cost-efficient.

Your hardware dealer carries a wide variety of screening, which you will use for one of two basic types of screen guard. You could use screening or metal fencing to construct a barbed-wire-style net over the entire skylight, but that's a lot of work, and the finished result is uglier than a weekend in Cleveland.

There is a better way! Like all the other projects in this book, your screen guard has to follow three rules: it must be inexpensive, easy-to-build, *and* look great. This solution meets these criteria on the basis of simplicity alone.

When you are building the plate-style skylight, before you install the glass or Plexiglas itself, simply lay a piece of ½" screening over the glass. *Then* install the aluminum angle and caulk. The screen fits snugly between the aluminum angle and the skylight material, and looks like a custom job. This type of screen guard has only two minor drawbacks: first, it works only with the plate-style skylight (though that shouldn't be much of a problem, since you probably wouldn't put screening over a pre-fab bubble); second, it makes outside cleaning a little more difficult, although still not a major chore. But meanwhile, the guard will protect your skylight from damage without costing you much time or money.

CLEANING

Occasionally, your skylight will need to be cleaned. Use your own discretion for setting up a cleaning schedule. The outside can be hosed off with water regardless of the skylight material. Use a glass cleaner (such as Windex) for the inside.

For Plexiglas skylights, your Plexiglas dealer can recommend a high-quality polymer protector that functions much like car wax, forming a protective barrier to keep dirt and moisture from accumulating on the Plexiglas. Make sure you get a protector that's compatible with the surface you're using. Conventional wax, for instance, would dull Plexiglas.

If you are using anything other than plain water or a specifically recommended cleaner, be certain the cleaner is non-abrasive, so it doesn't scratch the surface.

Finally, clean the inside of the shaftway walls. And unless the skylight is in the kitchen

Plasticrafts translucent dome admits light while preserving privacy for a home overshadowed by taller buildings.

or bathroom, where it's more apt to pick up moisture and dirt than in other rooms, you need do this task only occasionally.

That's all there is to it! No filters to change, no batteries to buy, no hoses or belts to wear out. Go ahead and enjoy your skylight—you deserve it!

Appendix

One advantage of building your own skylight is that the materials are so easily available. To make the skylights described in this book, you need go to only three or four places: a lumberyard, a hardware or houseware store, and a glass or plastic supply store. And you can locate everything by using the Yellow Pages. For a list of manufacturers outside your local area, consult *Sweet's Architectural Catalog File for Design and Construction of General Building* (about 20 volumes, all indexed) in the Business, Science, or Industry department of your library. This set of books contains almost every maker of anything needed in the building trades.

Manufactured skylights cost three to four times as much as the ones you can build, but come in standard sizes, minimizing the carpentry needed to install them. Some of the shapes available are the dome, box, square pyramid, and triangular pyramid. They come in two basic colors—neutral gray and bronze—and in five densities for each color from light to dark. Some can be purchased with a frame that allows it to be opened up.

Before you purchase a skylight, make sure the unit you're considering has these features:

1. The skylight should have an inner and outer shell to create the dead air space necessary to insulate the skylight.
2. The aluminum angle should have welded corners that are thick enough to be rigid and firm.
3. The sealant for the skylight should be a silicone or polysulfide type. Ask to make sure.
4. Ask how the skylight is to be fastened to the curb. If the procedure seems too difficult, then look elsewhere, as there are superb skylights which attach to the curb easily.

When it came time for us to gather a list of skylight manufacturers, we did what most of you would do: contact the companies to see what they had to offer. Below you will find an alphabetized listing of the manufacturers who responded to our inquiry, together with the types of products they feature.

CODE TO SKYLIGHT FEATURES: AC—accessories, CD—ceiling domes, CO—custom units only, F—flashing, II—instructions included, IU—insulating units, SF—self-flashing, SG—safety glass, V—venting unit.

APC Corporation
P.O. Box 515
50 Utter Ave.
Hawthorne, NJ 07507
(201) 423-2900
AC, CD, F, V

Bristol Fiberlite Industries
401 E. Goetz Ave.
Santa Ana, CA 92707
(714) 540-8950
CD, IU, SF

Dilworth Manufacturing Co.
Box 158
Honey Brook, PA 19344
(717) 354-8956
CD, F. Limited, but nice, line of curb-mounted skylights.

Fisher Skylights, Inc.
50 Snake Hill Rd.
West Nyack, NY 10994
(914) 358-9000
F, IU, SG, V. Wide range of conventional and unusual skylight products tailored to business applications; impressive list of corporate clients.

Hillsdale Industries, Inc.
5049 S. National Dr.
Knoxville, TN 37914
(615) 637-1711
CD, IU, V. Residential and commercial units available.

IGS
Imperial Glass Structures Co.
2120 S. Foster Ave.
Wheeling, IL 60090
(312) 253-6150
CO, F, IU. Skylight products for businesses; wide range of corporate clients.

Lynbrook Glass and Architectural Metals Corp.
941 Motor Parkway
Hauppauge, NY 11787
(516) 582-3060
F, IU, SG, V.

Naturalite, Inc.
3233 West Kingsley Rd.
Garland, TX 75040
(214) 278-1354
AC, F, IU, V. Good selection of home skylights.

Plastic Sales & Manufacturing, Inc.
3030 Cherry St.
Kansas City, MO 64108
(816) 561-7050
CD, F, IU, SF, V. Nice catalog and selection; some unusual dome shapes.

Plasticrafts, Inc.
600 W. Bayaud St.
Denver, CO 80223
(303) 744-3701
CD, F, II, IU. Esoteric designs, as well as technically oriented specifications and instructions.

Rainbow Skylights
P.O. Box 10298
Houston, TX 77206
(713) 695-1687
F, II, IU, SF, SG, V. Nice selection of residential skylights; informative brochure.

Rollamatic Roofs, Inc.
1400 Yosemite Ave.
San Francisco, CA 94124
(415) 822-5655
CO, V. Custom units for homes and businesses.

Super Sky Products, Inc.
P.O. Box 47
Thiensville, WI 53092
(414) 242-2000
CD, F, IU, SG. Wide range of conventional and unusual skylight products tailored toward businesses.

Wasco Products, Inc.
P.O. Box 351
Sanford, ME 04073
(207) 324-8060
AC, CD, II, IU, SG, V. Wide range of home products, along with clear instructions and illustrations.

Glossary

aluminum angle   Sheet aluminum already bent at a 90° angle. Comes in lengths up to 12 feet, and in a variety of widths.

amp rating   A measure of current flow in an electrical motor. Best used in combination with the horsepower rating to judge the work capacity of power tools.

batten   Narrow strip of wood nailed around the top of the *curb* (which see); used as a spacer to maintain the correct distance between the aluminum angle and the skylight material.

bottom plate   The base piece of studding that the vertical support members are nailed to.

common nails   See *nails.*

corner bead   Pre-formed metal strip, used to reinforce corners when hanging drywall before the paste is applied.

corner buck   Assembly of lumber in the corner of a shaftway to serve as a *nail block* (see below).

curb   Wooden framework, usually made of 2" x 6" lumber, used to frame the skylight material and give it a suitable base.

drywall   A kind of *gypsum board* (which see) — a wall covering used on interior walls. Drywall is available in large sheets, 4' x 10' and 4' x 12'.

epoxy   Two-part adhesive which, when mixed together, forms a very strong bond between the materials being joined.

flashing   Material, usually aluminum, used in roof and wall construction to protect against water seepage. Flashing comes in widths from 6" to 18" and can be bought in any length.

framing   The skeletal structure of walls, floors, and roofs, formed by nailing lumber together.

galvanizing   A way of treating steel — for example, nails — against rust.

gasket   Any object used to create an airtight seal between two materials.

gypsum board   Material made from gypsum, sandwiched between two layers of heavy paper. It comes in standard sizes, usually 4' x 8', 4' x 10', and 4' x 12'; and in thicknesses from $\frac{3}{8}$" to $\frac{3}{4}$", in $\frac{1}{8}$" increments. *Drywall* (which see), Sheetrock, and plasterboard are kinds of gypsum board.

header   A beam placed perpendicular to *joists* (see below), to which the joists are nailed; used to frame an opening such as a skylight. It is also used as a lintel for a door or window.

joist   One of a series of parallel beams used to support floors and ceilings.

nail blocks   Also called *nailers*. Pieces of wood installed in the *framing* to provide a place to nail wall or ceiling covering to. Nail blocks are quite frequently used in the corners of the stud walls.

nailers   See *nail blocks.*

nails   Range in size from 2d to 60d. See *penny. Common* nails have large flat heads, while *finish* nails have a small head that makes them easy to countersink.

one-by-   Term for lumber measurement; used for any board whose width dimension is not critical, but whose thickness is. One-by- material comes standard in most lumberyards in widths from 2" to 12", in 2" increments. See *two-by-.*

opaque   Said of a material (such as stone or wood) that allows no light to pass through it. People often say "opaque" when they mean "translucent."

penny   Measurement for the length and corresponding diameter of a nail. The symbol for a penny is a lower case *d*. The larger the number, the larger the nail (e.g. 8d, 12d, 16d).

plaster lathe   Building material made from gypsum and fastened to the frame of a building. This material usually comes in 2'x 4' sections and is used as a base for a plaster wall.

plate glass   Tempered glass used for large window and door areas. It comes in a variety of thicknesses and is usually cut to size.

Plexiglas   Trademark of Rohm and Haas Co. The product — a high-impact-resistant, light-weight, weather-resistant acrylic plastic sheet — comes in clear (transparent), translucent, and opaque forms, and in a variety of sizes and thicknesses.

plywood   Laminated building material made of three or more layers of veneer joined with glue and usually laid with the grain of adjoining plies at right angles. The standard size of plywood is 4' x 8'; it comes in thicknesses from ⅛" to ¾" in ⅛" increments.

rafter   A structural roof member, designed to support roof loads.

roll insulation   A blanket of mineral fiber, such as rock or glass wool on kraft paper, with side tabs for fastening to the studs. Comes in thicknesses of 2", 3", 4", and 6", and in widths of 16" or 24".

Romex   Brand name for plastic-sheathed cable with solid copper conductors that can be used indoors or outdoors.

scaffold   A raised, temporary work platform made of wood or metal.

shaft or **shaftway**   In skylight construction, an open space connecting the roof and the ceiling that directs light to the room below.

sheathing   A covering over the studs or rafters, usually boards of plywood.

Sheetrock   See *gypsum board*.

shim   Small wedge-shaped pieces of wood, driven into tight spaces to make joints, hinges, molding, etc., fit more acccurately.

silicone caulk   Flexible sealant used to fill joints. Unaffected by water and temperature, its life expectancy is 20 years.

skylight material   As used in this book, the piece of transparent or translucent material (plate glass, Plexiglas, wire glass) that is set in the curb.

storm window (internal)   Thin sheet of Plexiglas fastened to a one-by-two on the inside perimeter of the curb. Its purpose is to create a dead air space for insulation.

stud   One of a series of vertical structural members, used for support in walls or partitions. Studs are usually two-by-threes or two-by-fours.

toenailing   Driving a nail at a slant so that it will penetrate a second surface it would not otherwise reach.

top plate   The top piece of studding to which the vertical support members of the wall are nailed.

translucent   Said of a material (such as milk glass or frosted glass) that allows light to pass through it, but through which no coherent image can be perceived. See *transparent*.

transparent   Said of a material (such as clear glass or Plexiglas) through which images can be perceived.

two-by-   Term for lumber measurement where the width is not critical but the thickness is. Two-by-material comes standard in most lumberyards in widths ranging from 3" to 12". See *one-by-*.

weatherstripping   Narrow sections of a thin material, such as brass or felt, used to prevent air flow around windows and doors.

wire glass   Two layers of plate glass reinforced by large-loop screening laminated between them.

wood screws   (W.S.) Screws threaded approximately two-thirds of their length. Available in steel, brass, or aluminum, they have a slotted or recessed (Phillips) head for turning.

Index